Edward Cordell:

The Complete Works

EDWARD CORDELL: THE COMPLETE WORKS

Edward Cordell:

The Complete Works

FOREWORD BY STEVEN J CORDELL

DEDICATION BY RICHARD J CORDELL

PHOTOGRAPHY and ARTIST BIOGRAPHY BY EILEEN W CORDELL

CURATED BY JULIA L CORDELL

FOR TED

CONTENTS

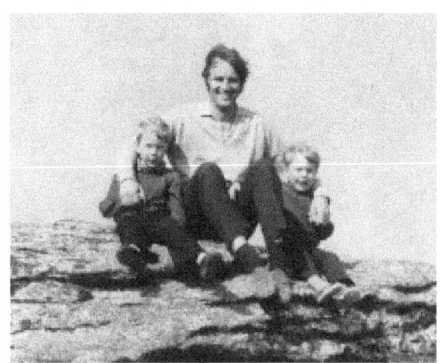

FOREWORD

This book represents the complete artistic works of my father, Edward John Cordell. He is certainly blessed with the gift of the artist, exhibiting a rare ability to capture the personality of his subjects, be they human or animal, landscape or still life; he is equally at home in pastel, charcoal, oil or watercolour, demonstrating the versatility of his talent.

However, as Emile Zola said, "The artist is nothing without the gift, but the gift is nothing without work".

Each of the pieces created by my father was usually the product of many hours, days and even weeks of painstaking work. Some might call it the pursuit of perfection, but for me it represents the essence of art – bringing something inanimate to life. This is why his family portraits, especially those of family pets, were so dearly appreciated by his clientele. Indeed, by creating a permanent image of his subjects, the artist effectively creates eternal life. So let this book in turn be an enduring tribute to the talent and work of the artist E.J. Cordell.

This book has been diligently compiled by Julia Cordell with the initial assistance of Eileen Cordell who found all the photographs of the original works. My deepest gratitude goes to Julia for having the idea and the patience to turn the idea into reality.

Steven

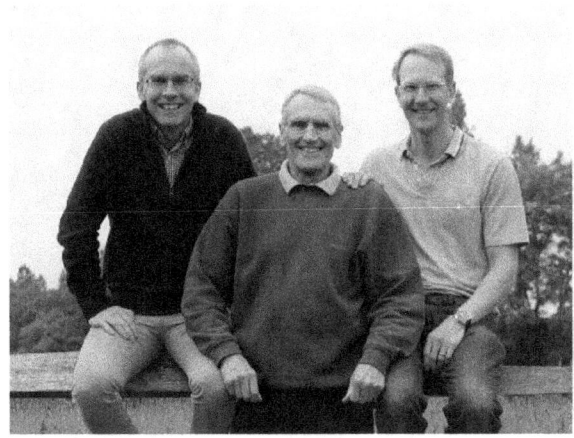

DEDICATION

Wonderful dad, husband, granddad, father-in-law, professional designer, adept sportsman and talented artist.

I always felt very proud to be able to say my father was an artist. Thank you for enriching our home with beautiful paintings throughout our lives.

I will always remember, fondly, you projecting slides on the wardrobe and working at your easel and asking our opinions on whether the eyes were right (as if we knew better than you).

I thank you for always offering good advice throughout my life; yours has always been the first opinion I would seek and, often, the only one required.

Without your guidance, wisdom and encouragement, I don't think I would have fulfilled my full potential. I thank you for being my greatest critic and my biggest fan.

I also thank my beautiful wife, Julia, for all the work she has put in to allow your paintings to be remembered and enjoyed forever.

I love you, Dad,

Richard

1 LANDSCAPES

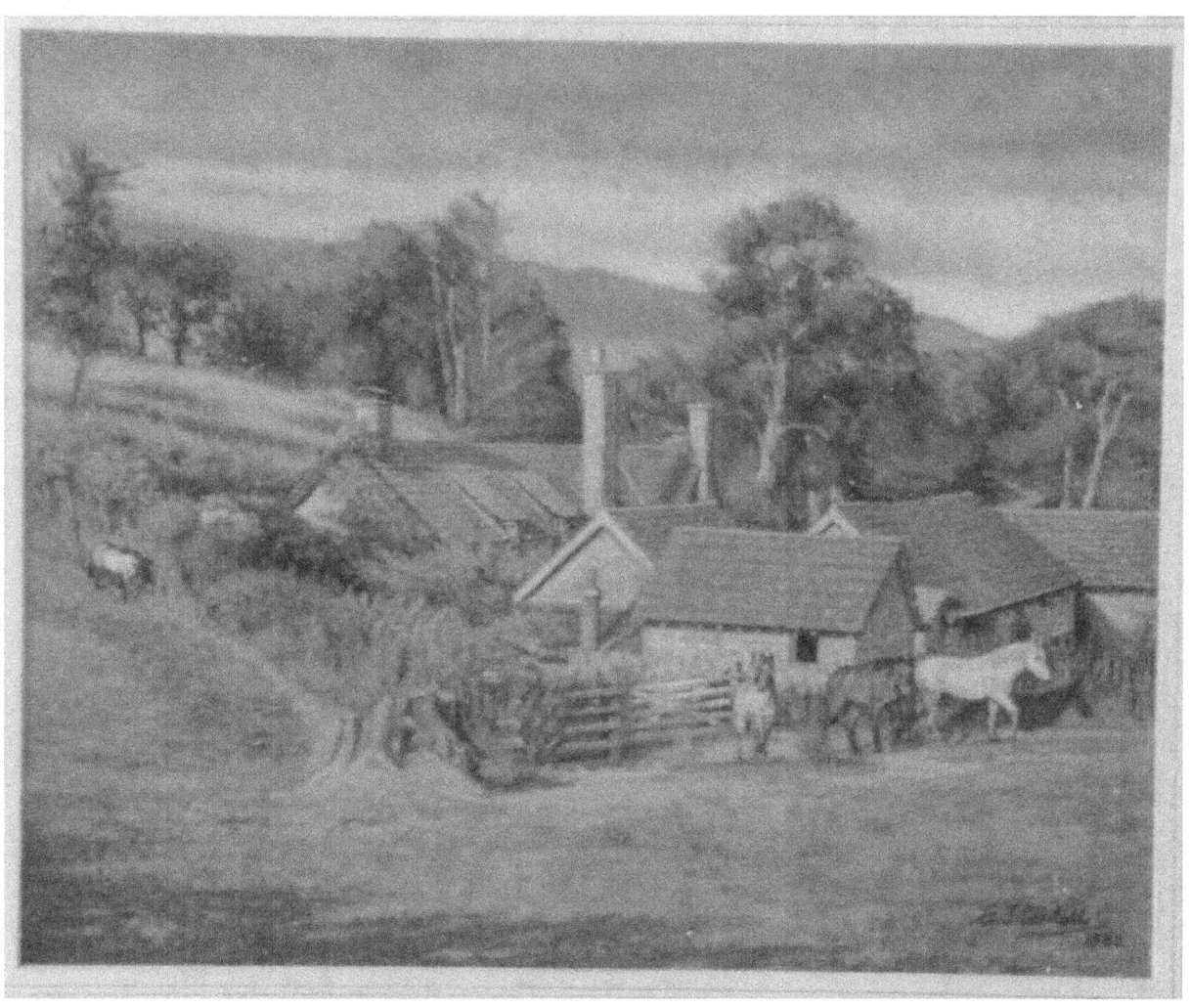

Farm near Porlock, 1979
m: pastel on paper

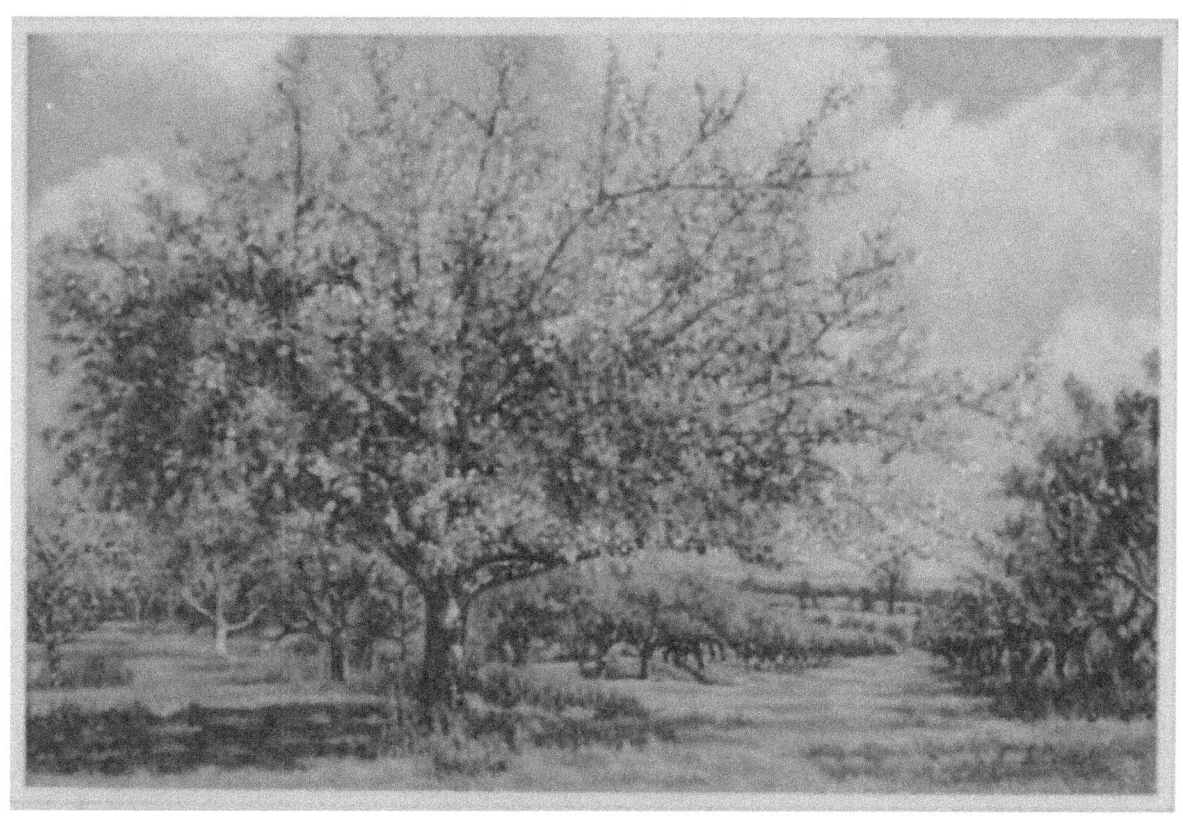

Apple blossoms in Pembury, 1981

m: watercolour on paper

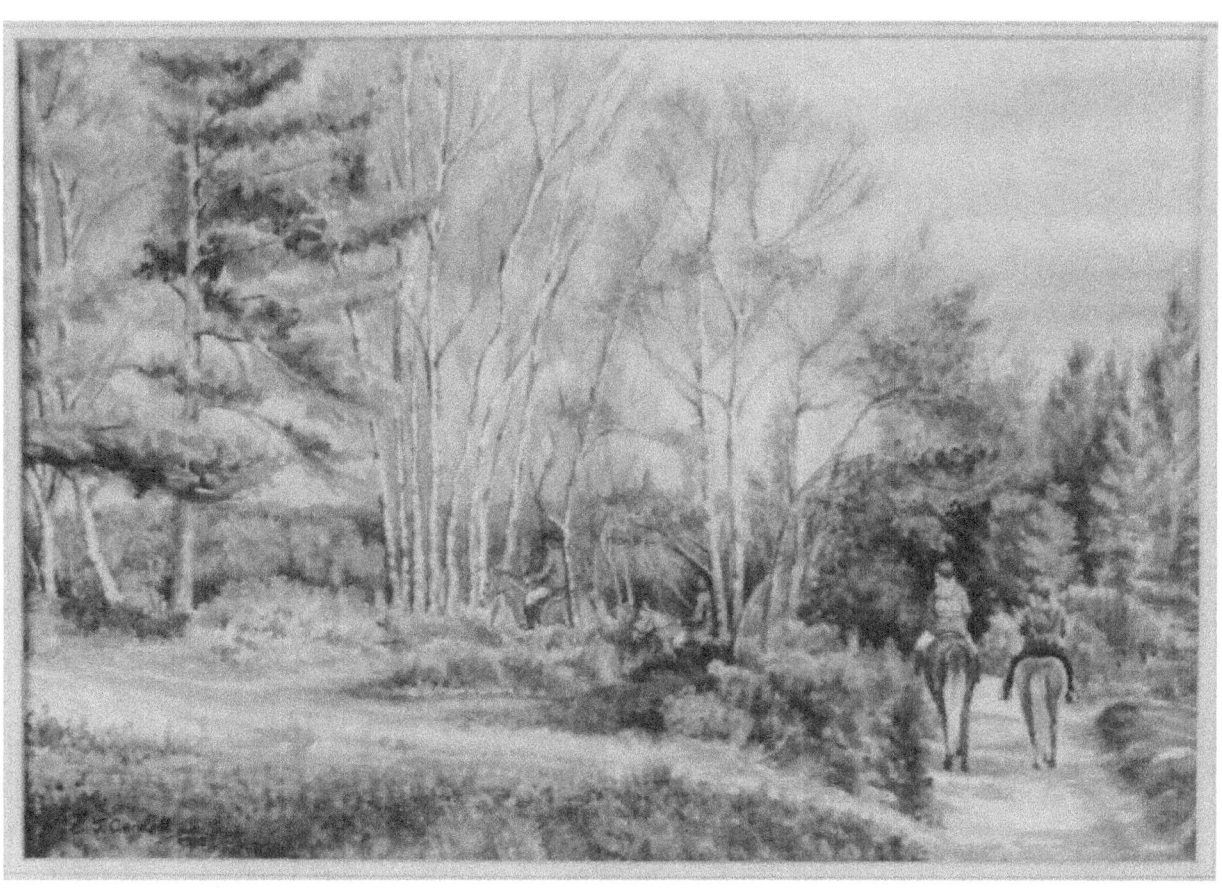

Riders in Pembury Walk, 1981

m: watercolour on paper

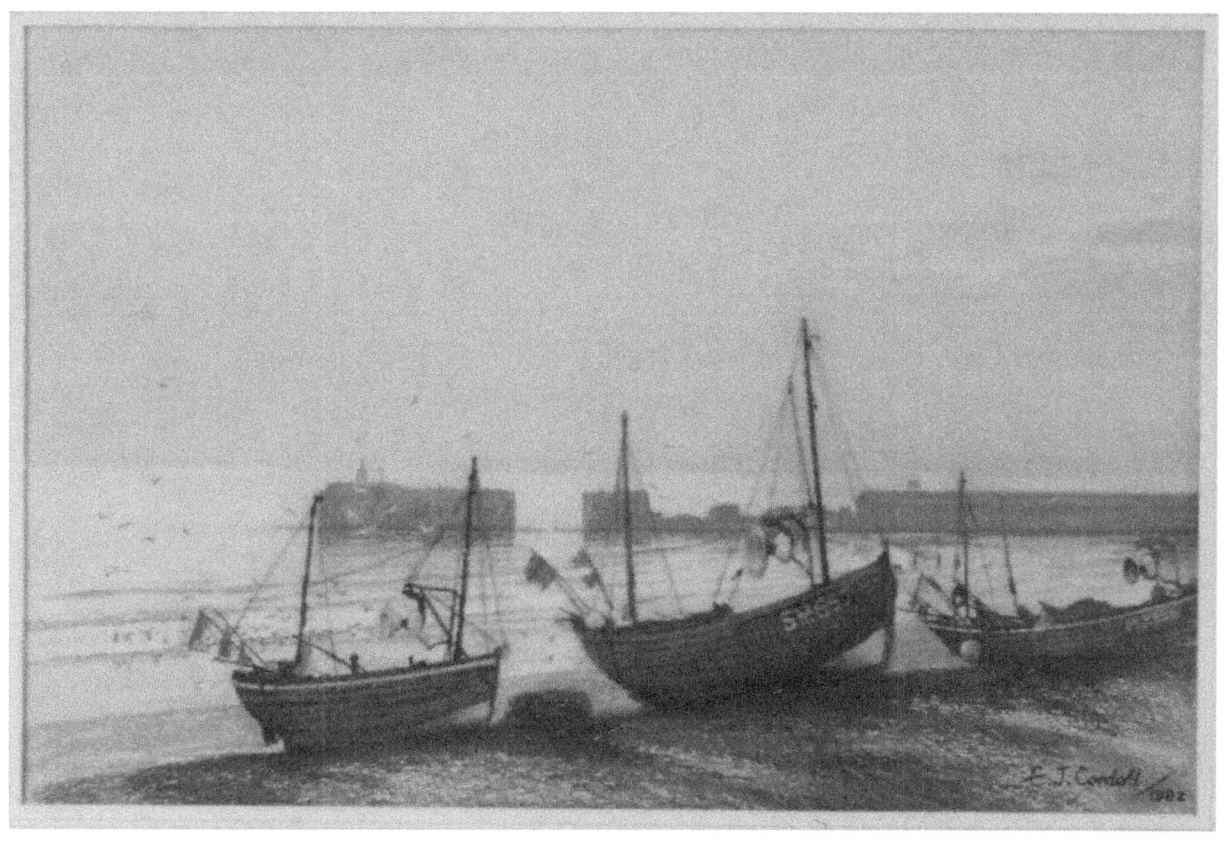

Boats at Hastings, 1982

m: pastel on paper

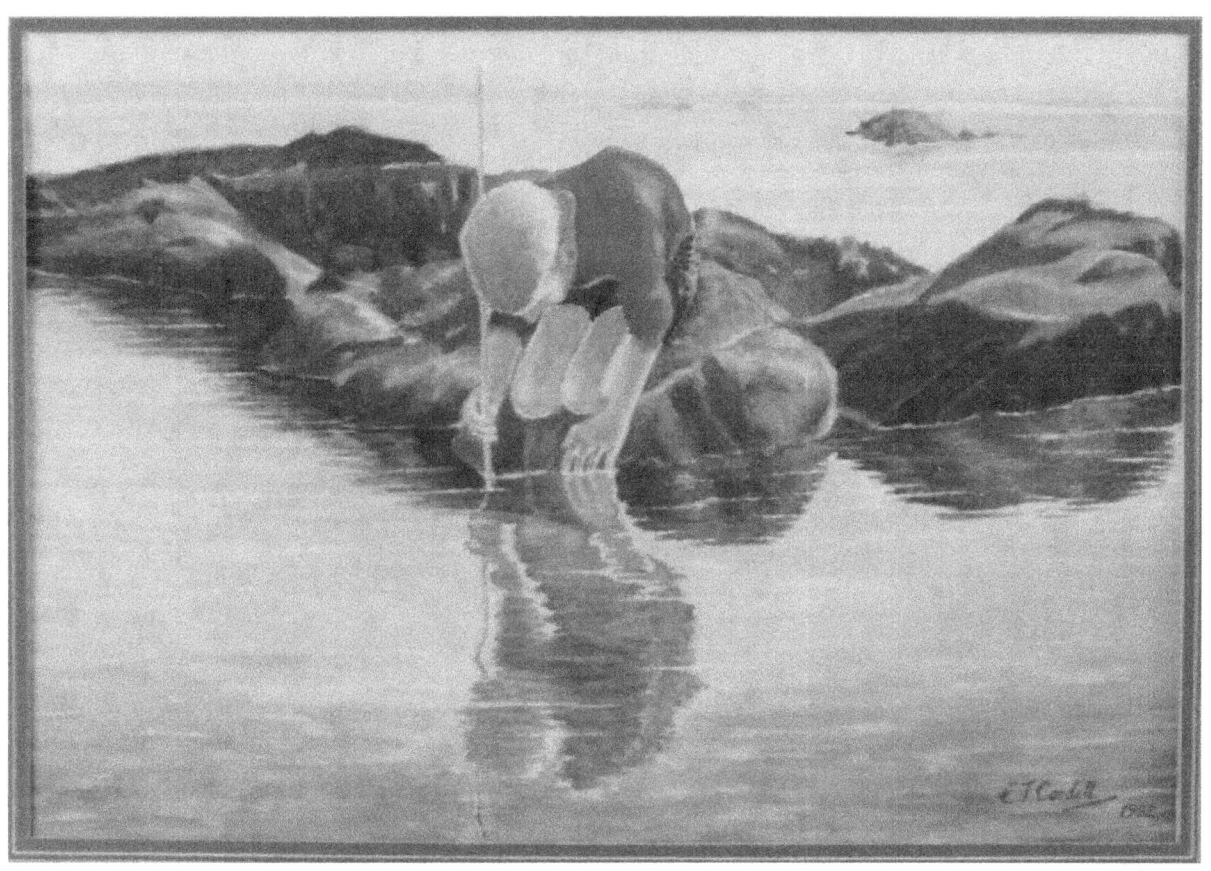

Rockpool in Looe, 1982

m: watercolour on paper

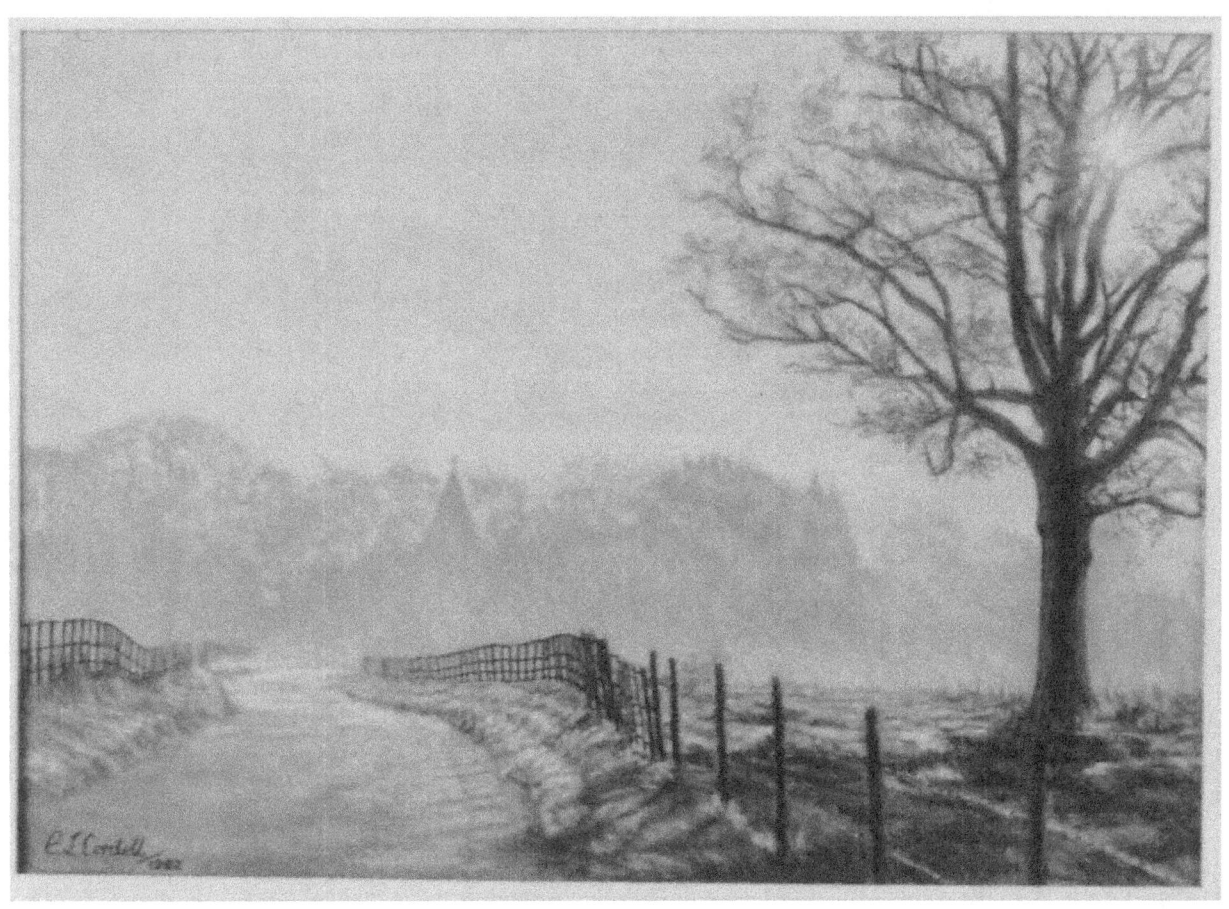

Pembury Old Church in winter, 1982

m: pastel on paper

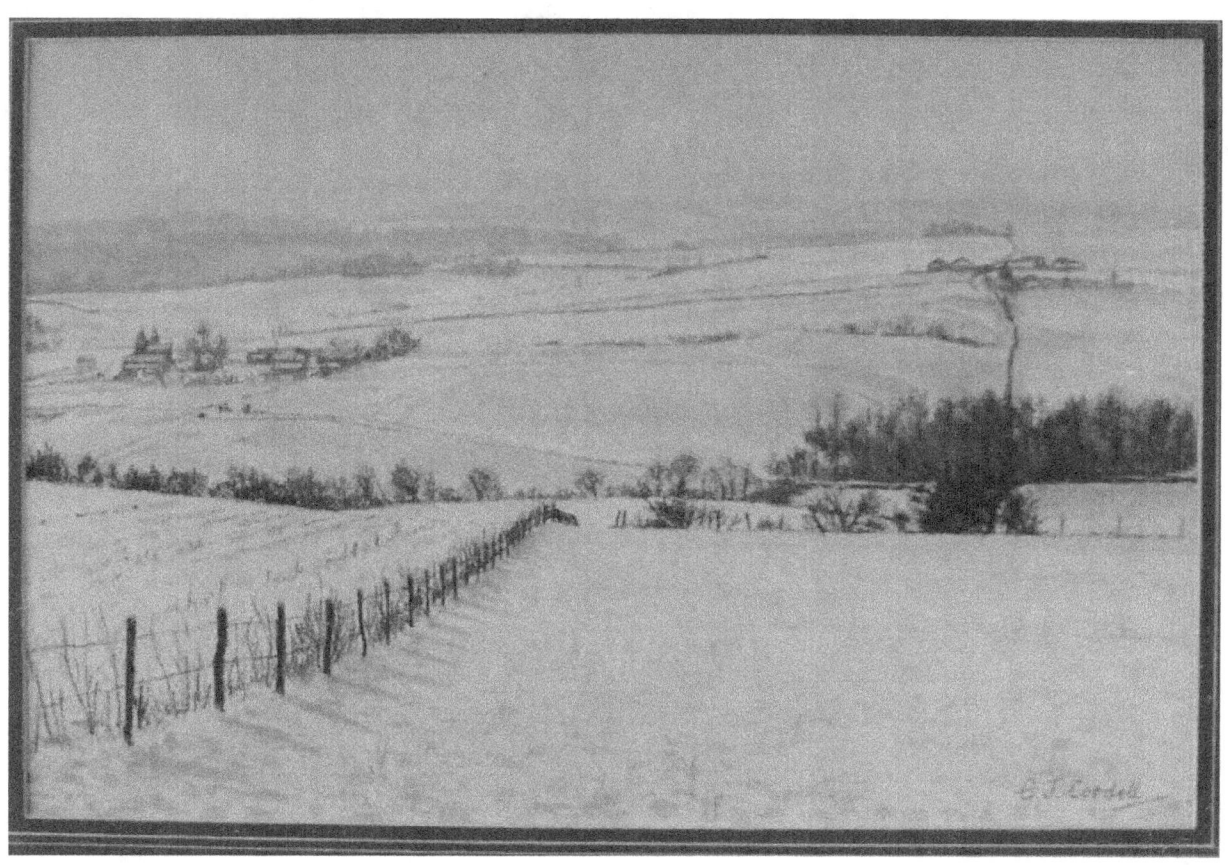

Snow scene in Pembury, 1982

m: pastel on paper

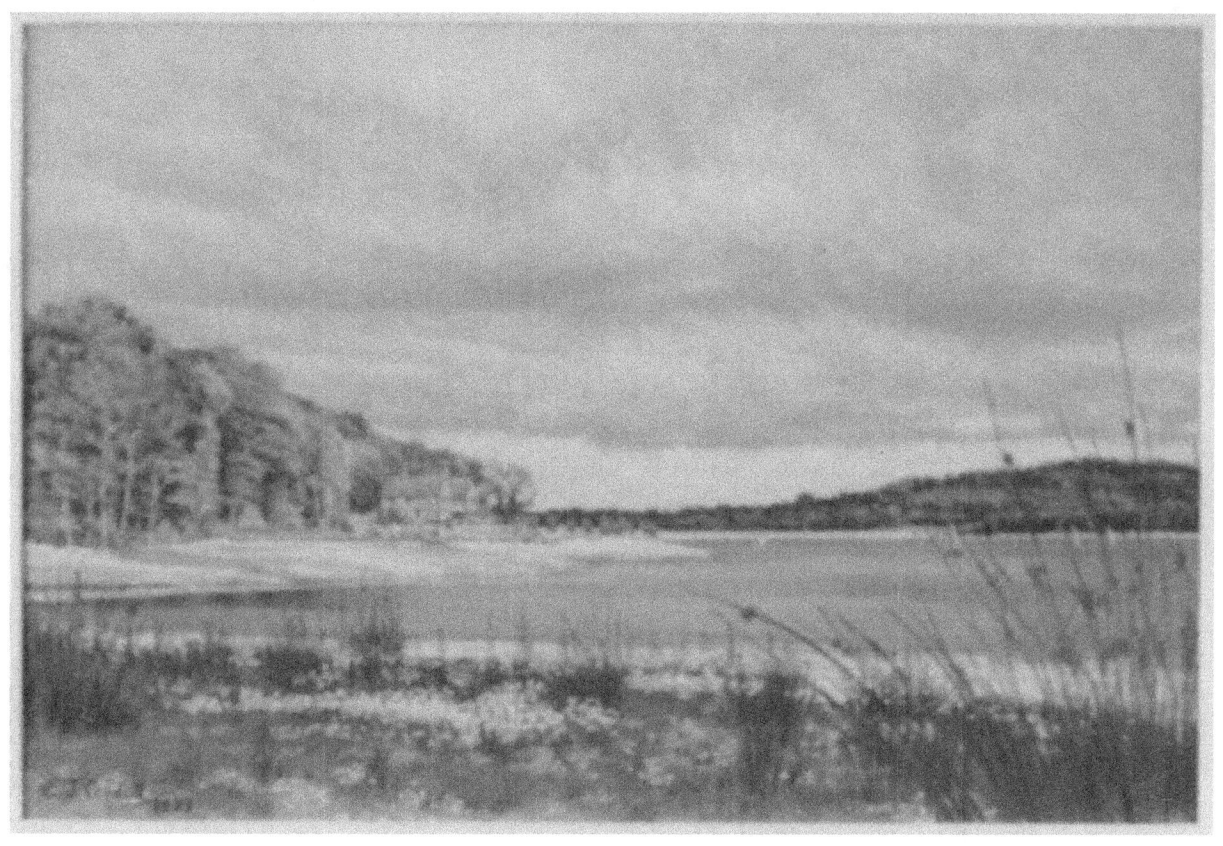

View of Bewl water, 1983
m: pastel on paper

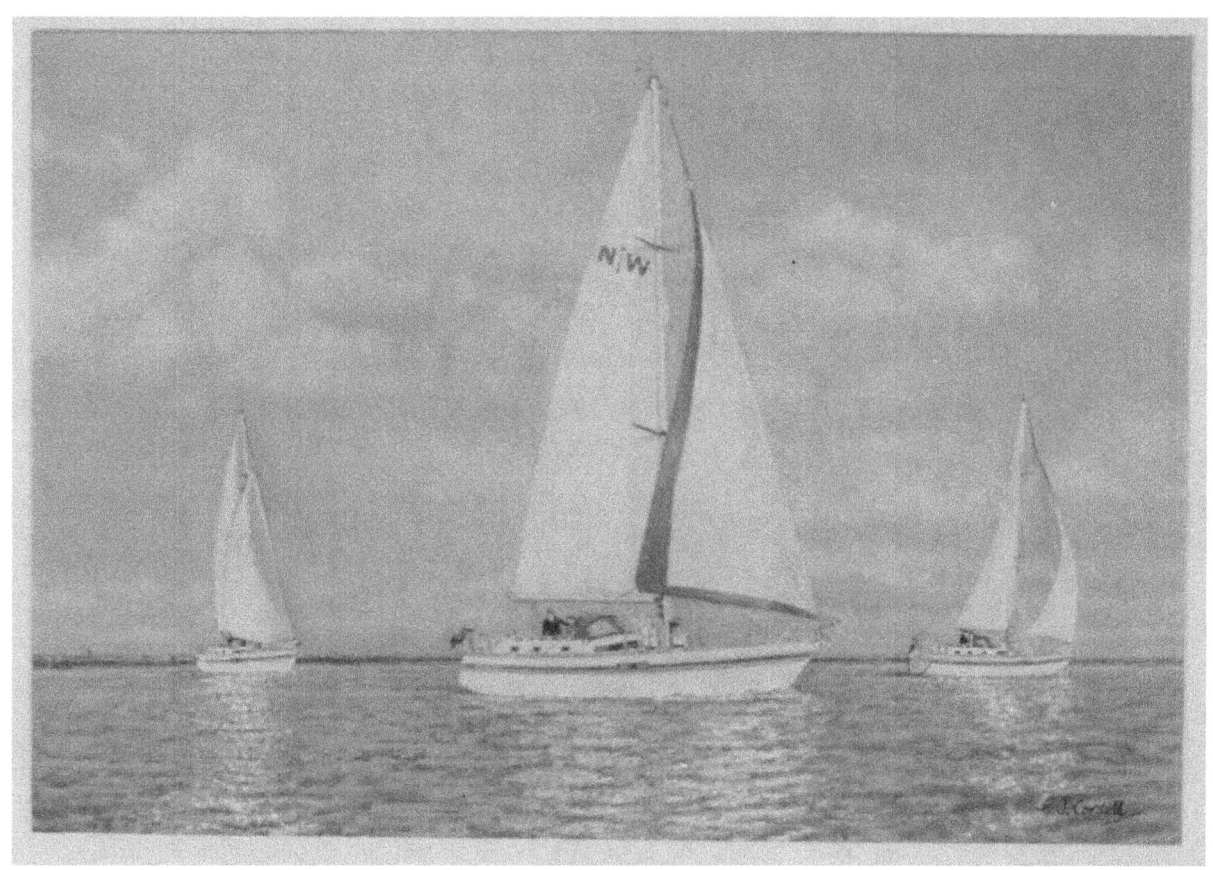

Francipam, date unknown

m: pastel on paper

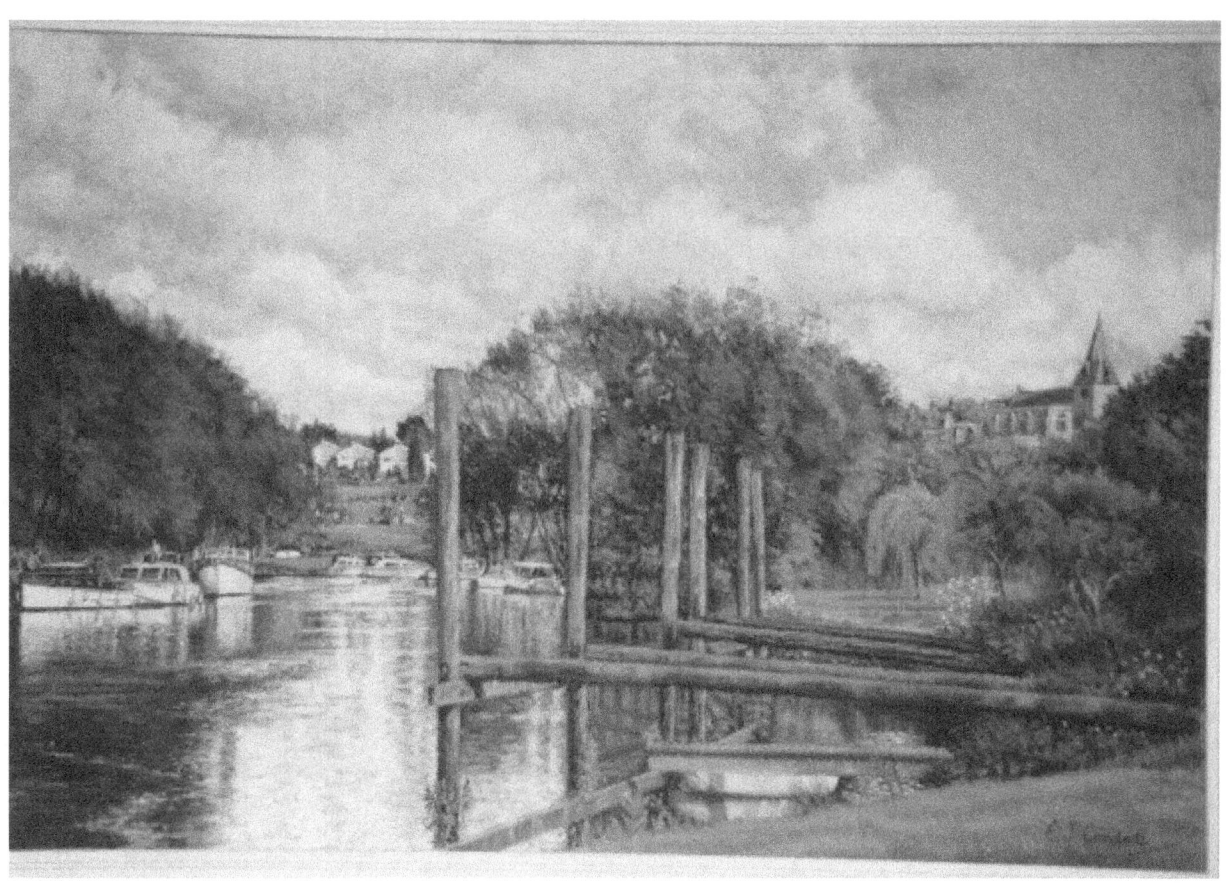

The Medway at Hartridge Farm, date unknown

m: pastel on paper

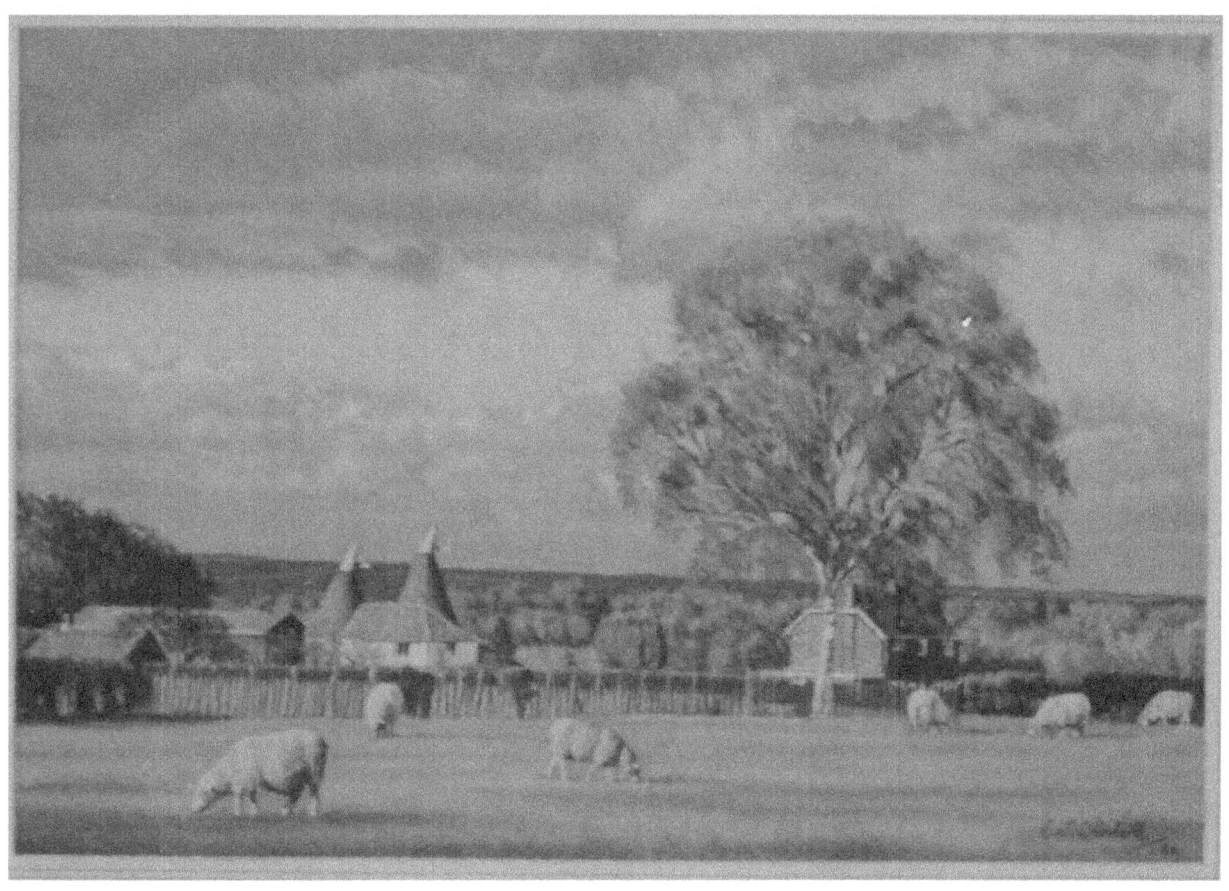

Lodge Farm in Matfield, 1984

m: pastel on paper

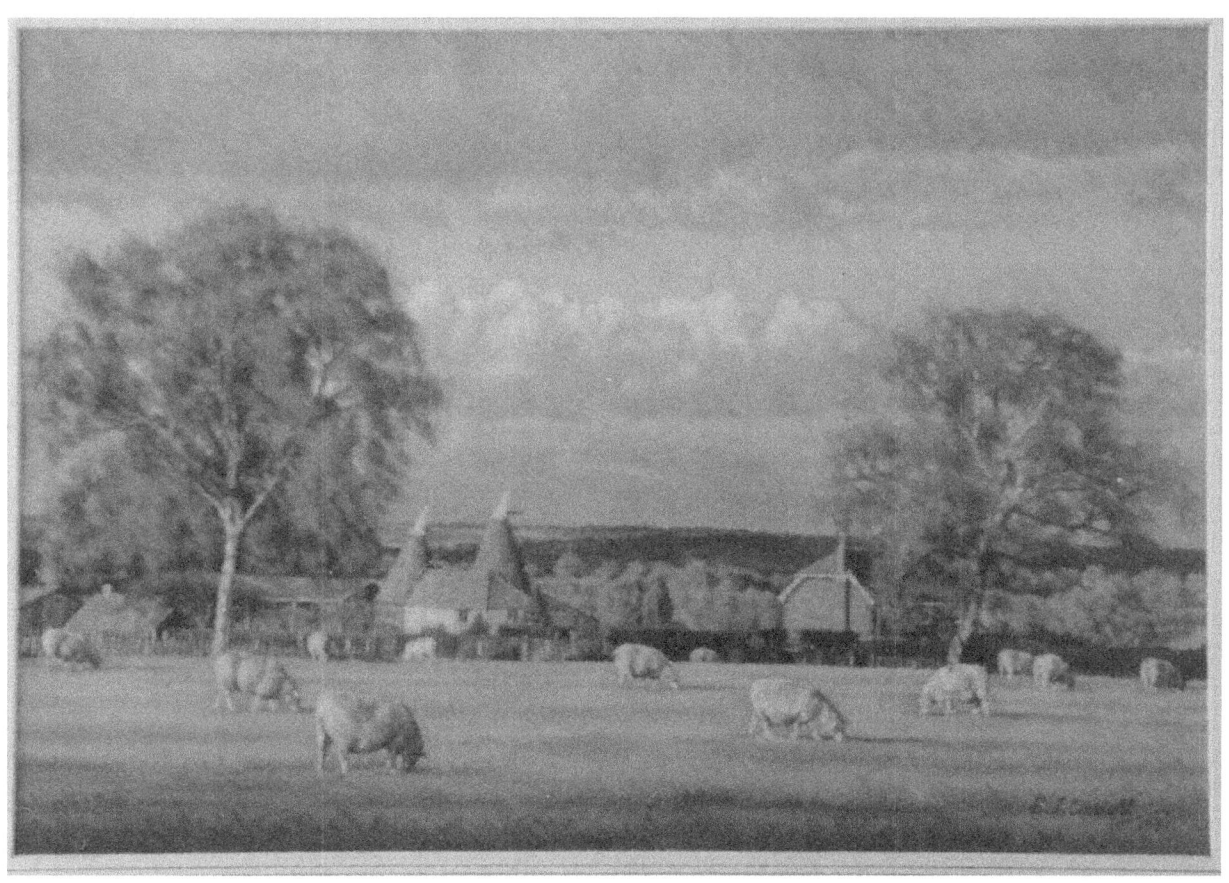

Lodge Farm in Matfield, 1987
m: pastel on paper

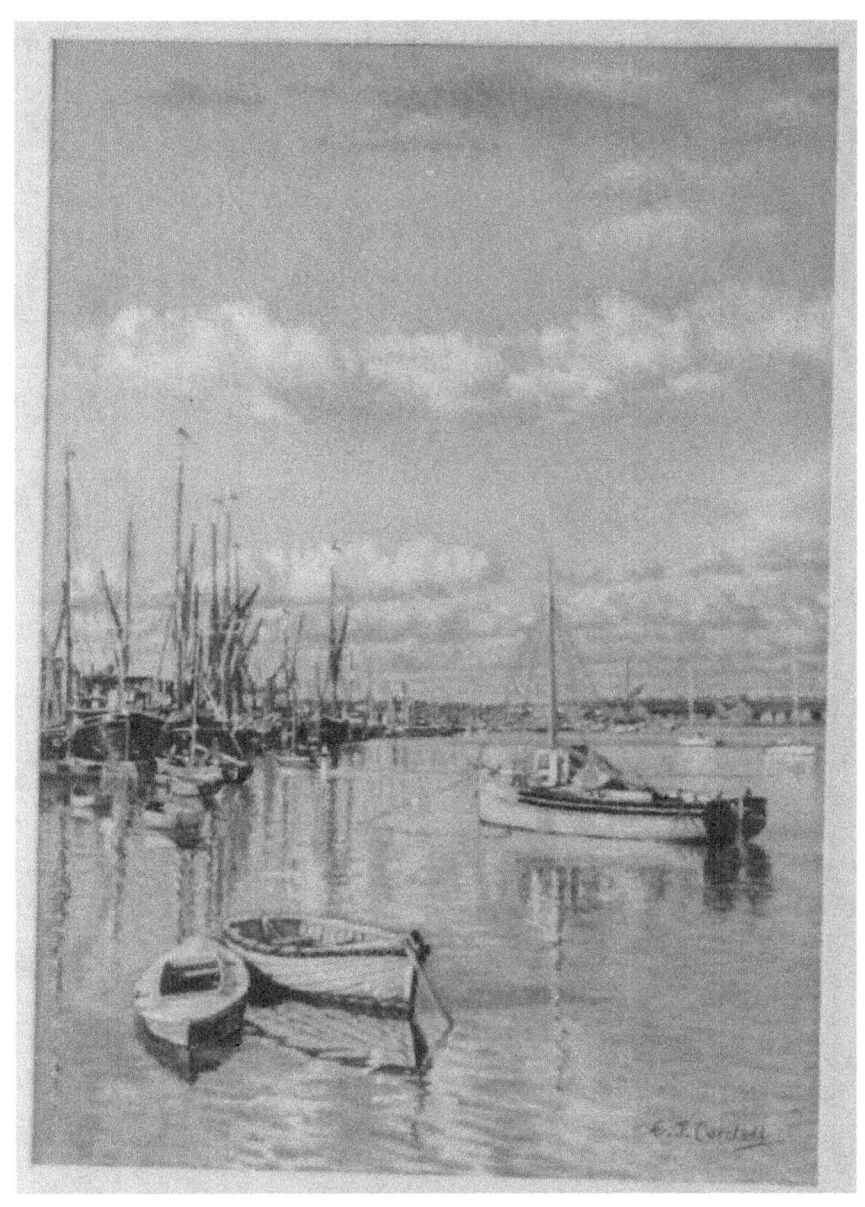

Barges and boats at Maldon, 1988
m: pastel on paper

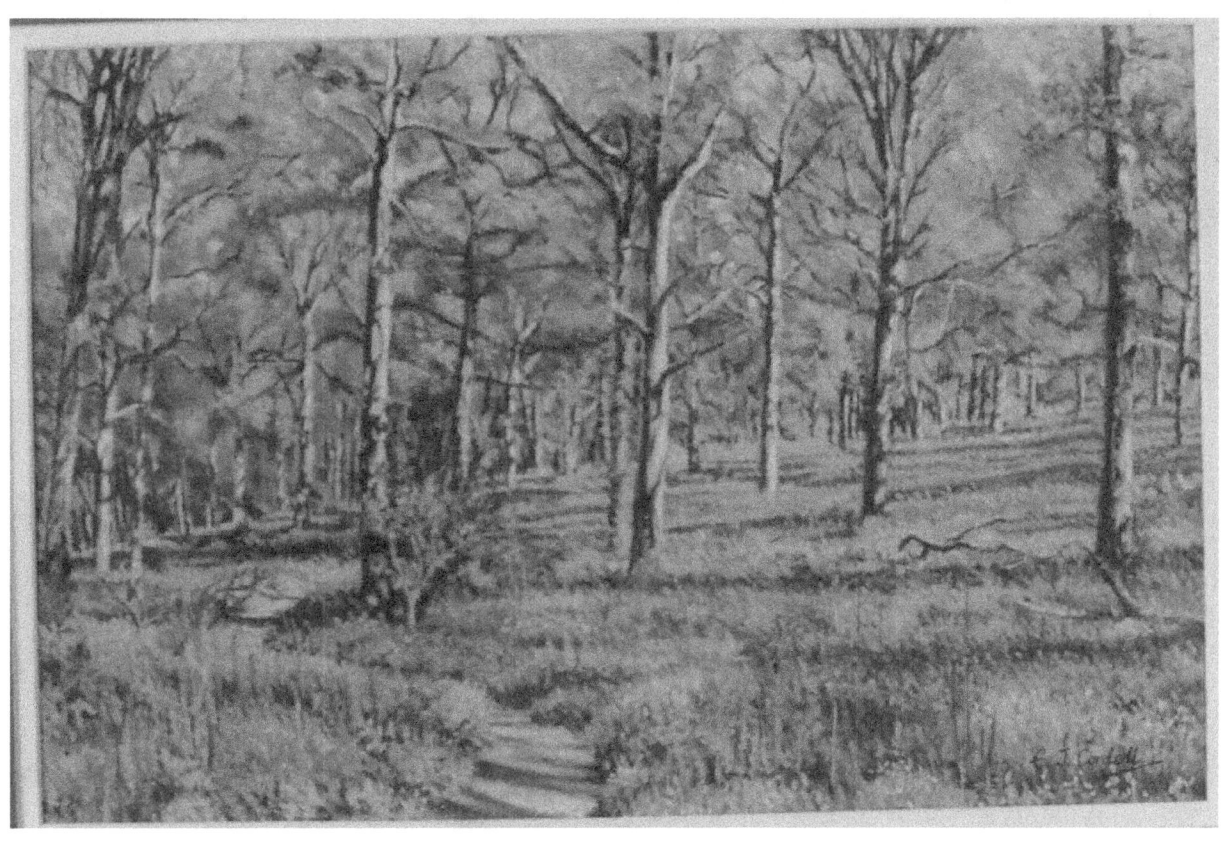

Bluebell Wood, 1988
m: pastel on paper

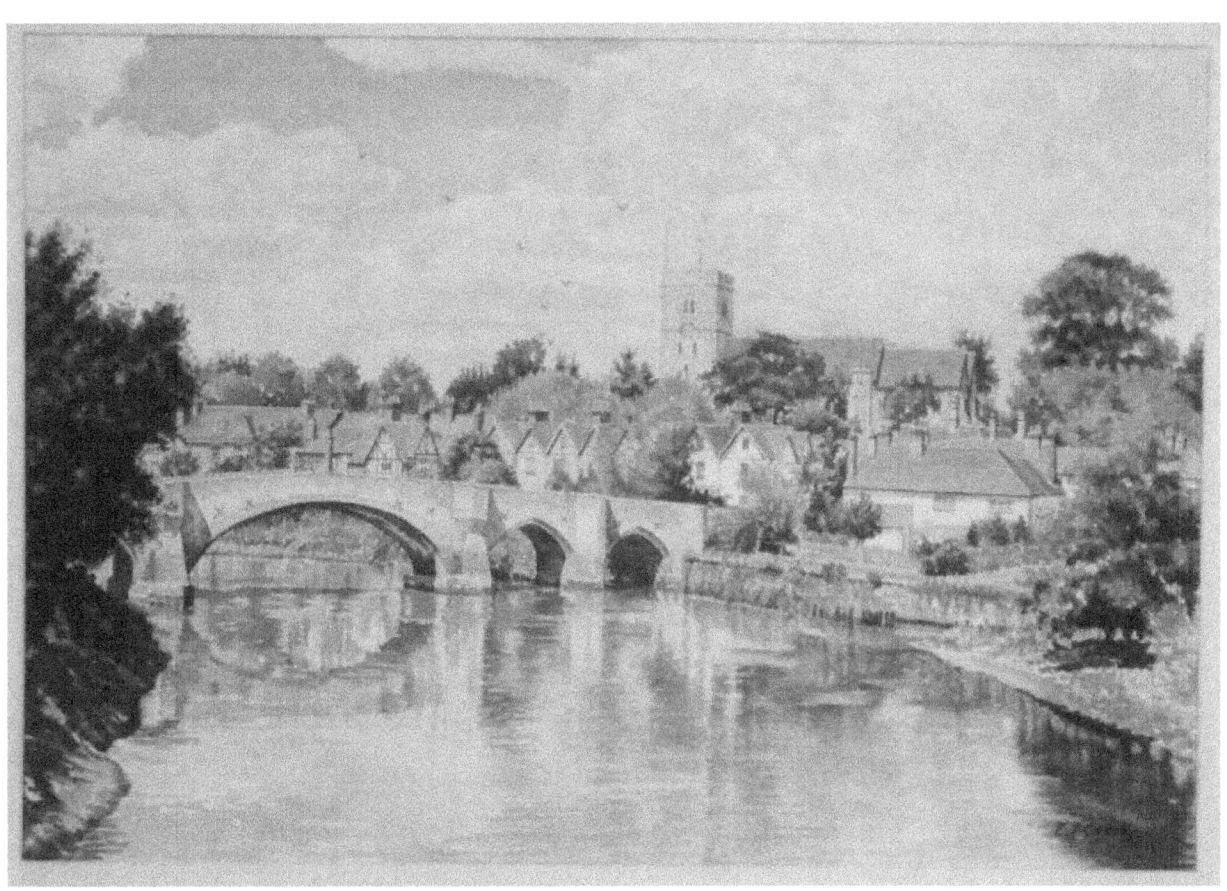

Aylesford Bridge in Kent, 1989

m: oil on canvas

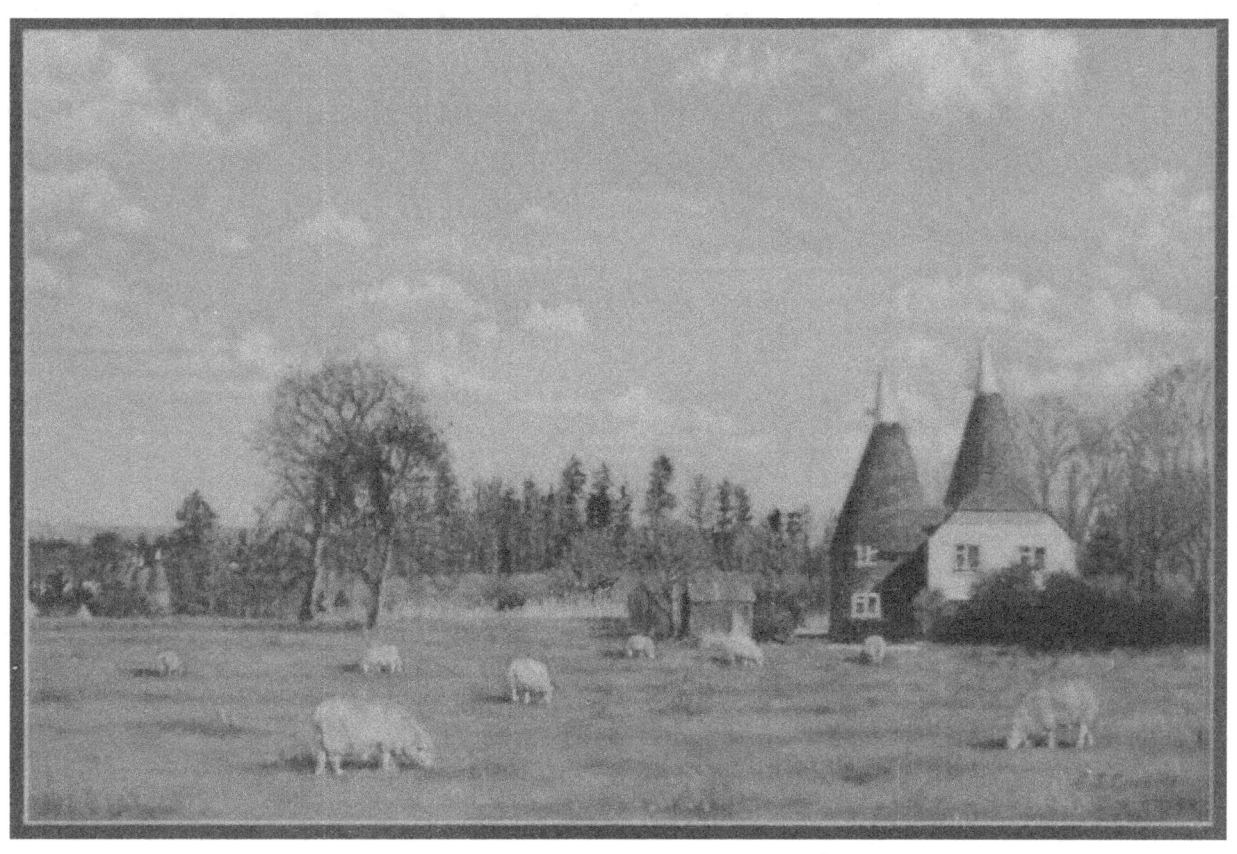

Oast house at Kippings Cross, 1989

m: pastel on paper

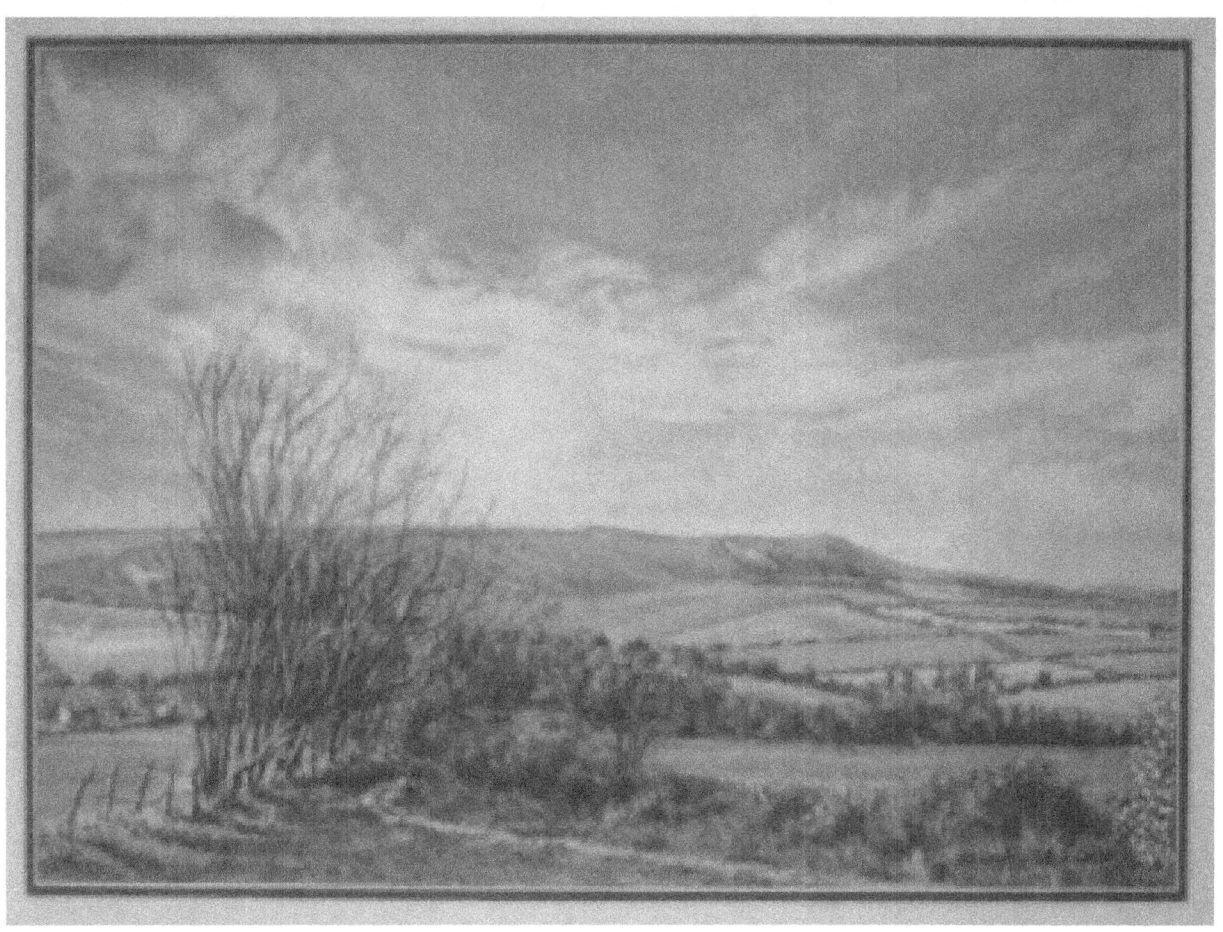

Firle Beacon in the South Downs, date unknown
m: pastel on paper

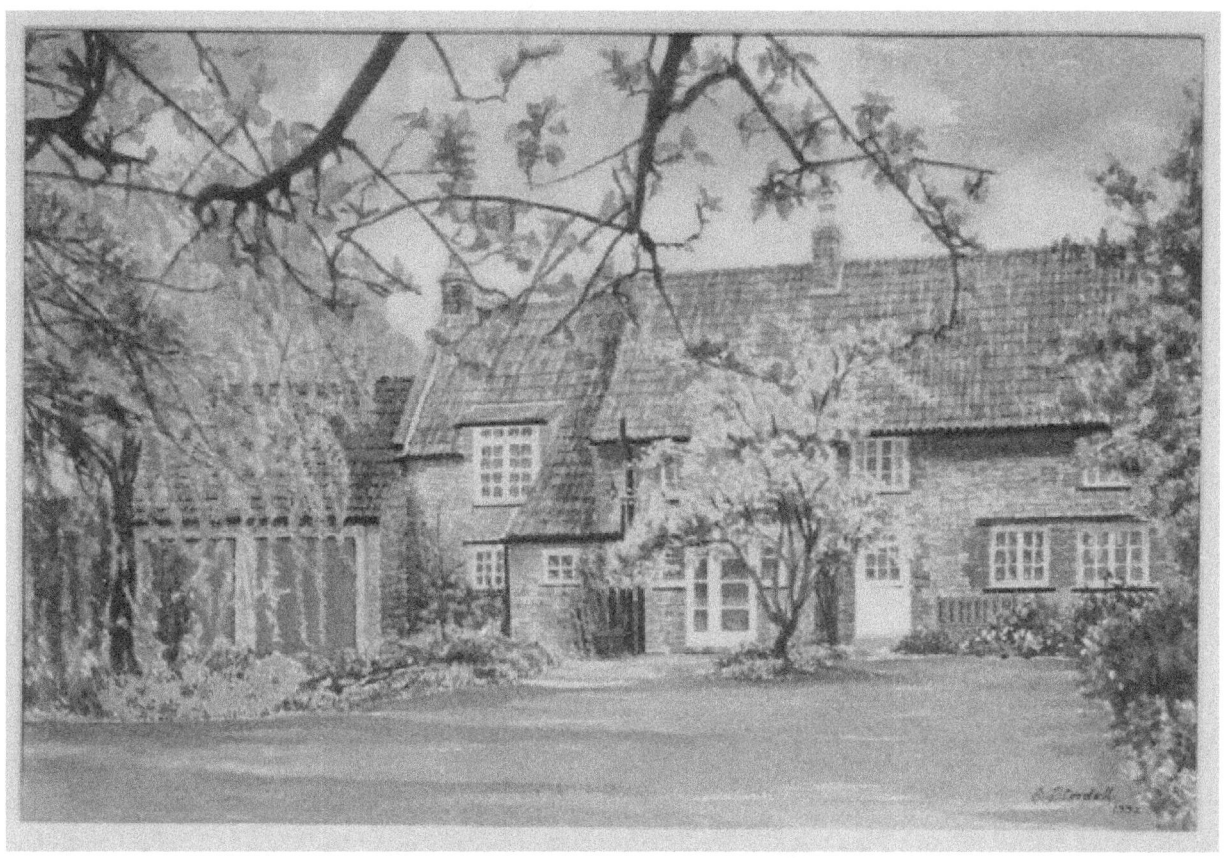

Sacha's house and garden, 1992

m: watercolour on paper

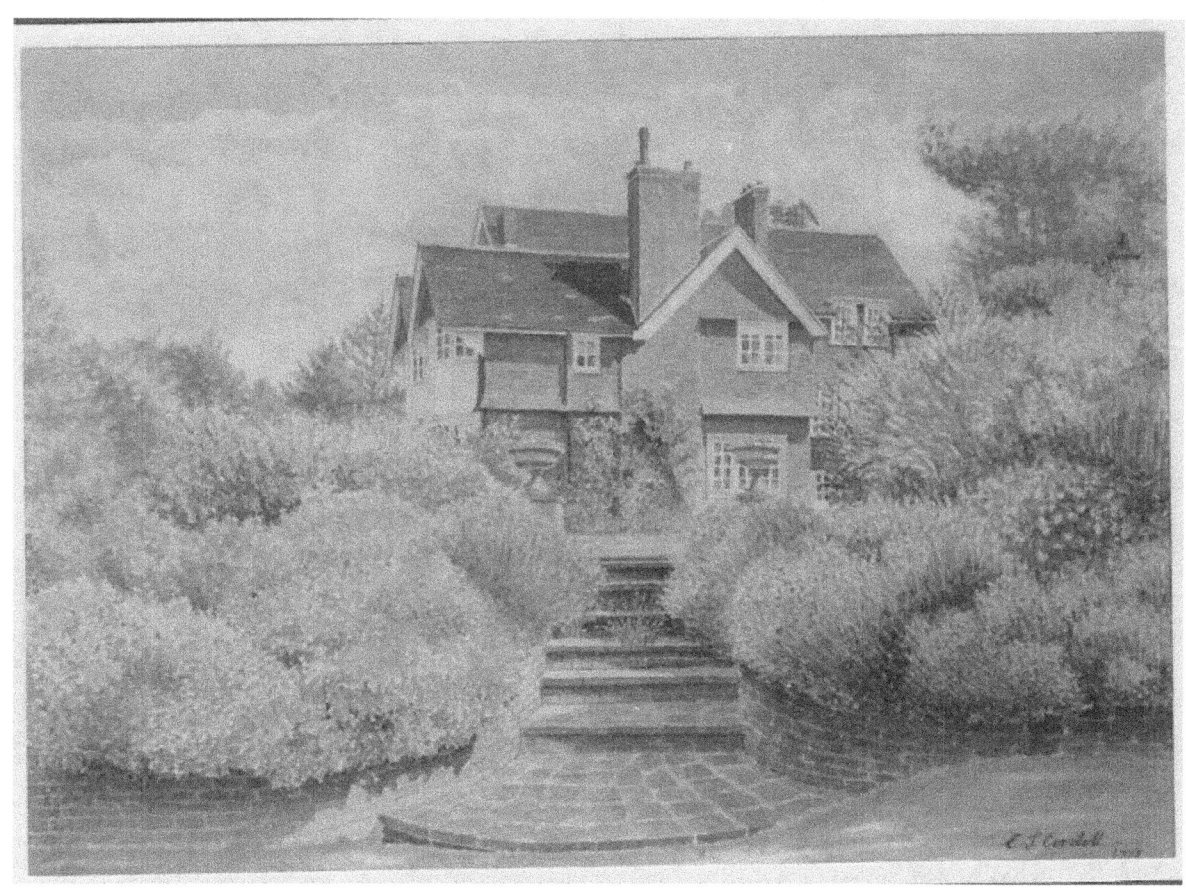

Gill and Bill's house in Essex, 1993

m: watercolour on paper

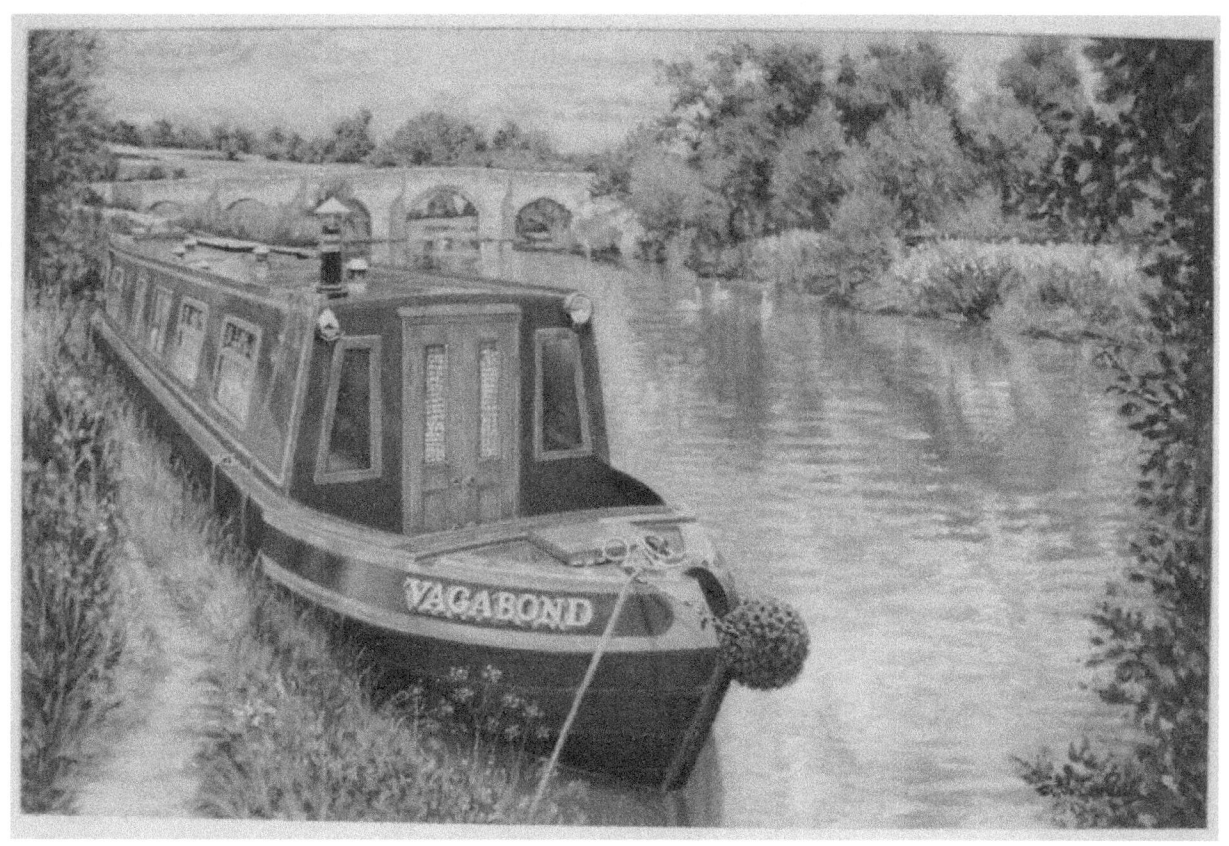

Vagabond on the River Medway in Kent, 1993

m: pastel on paper

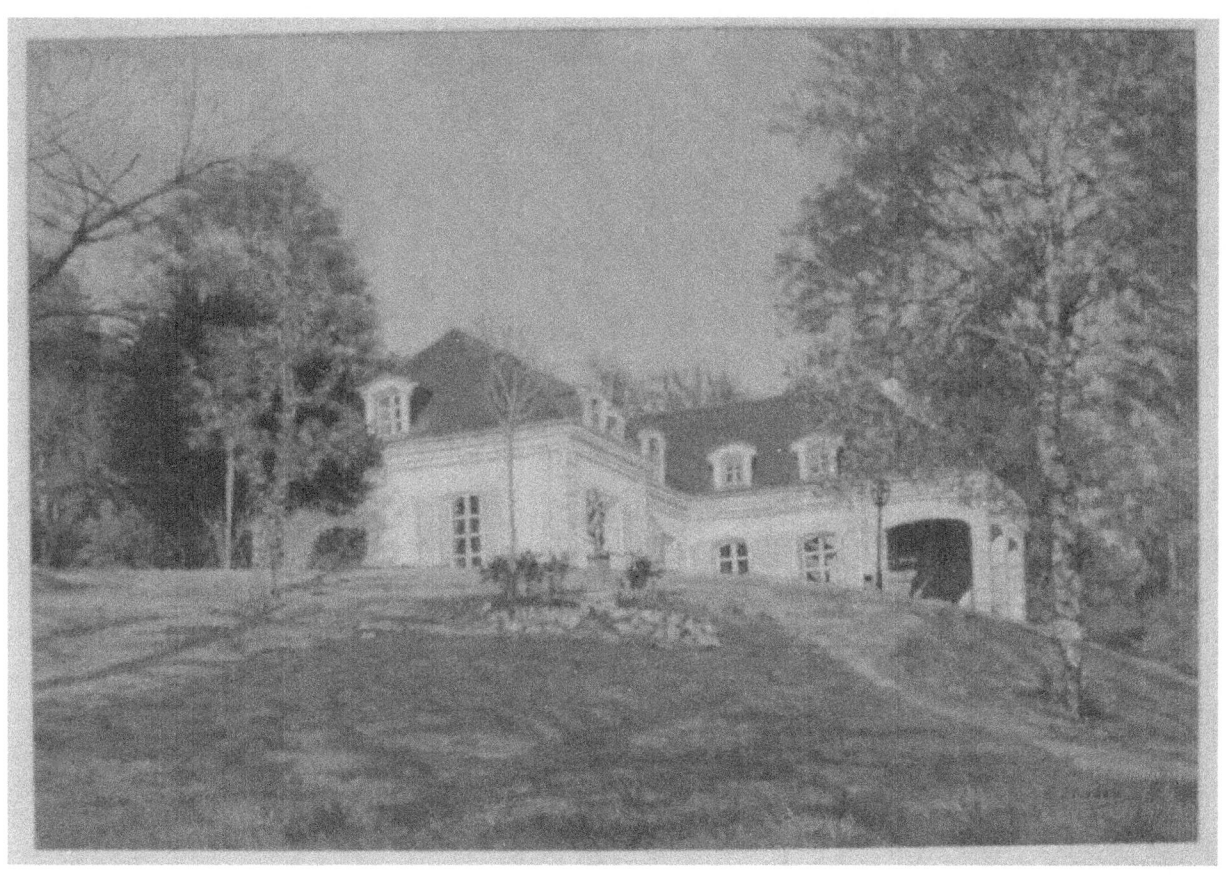

Keith and Pam's house in France, 1994

m: pastel on paper

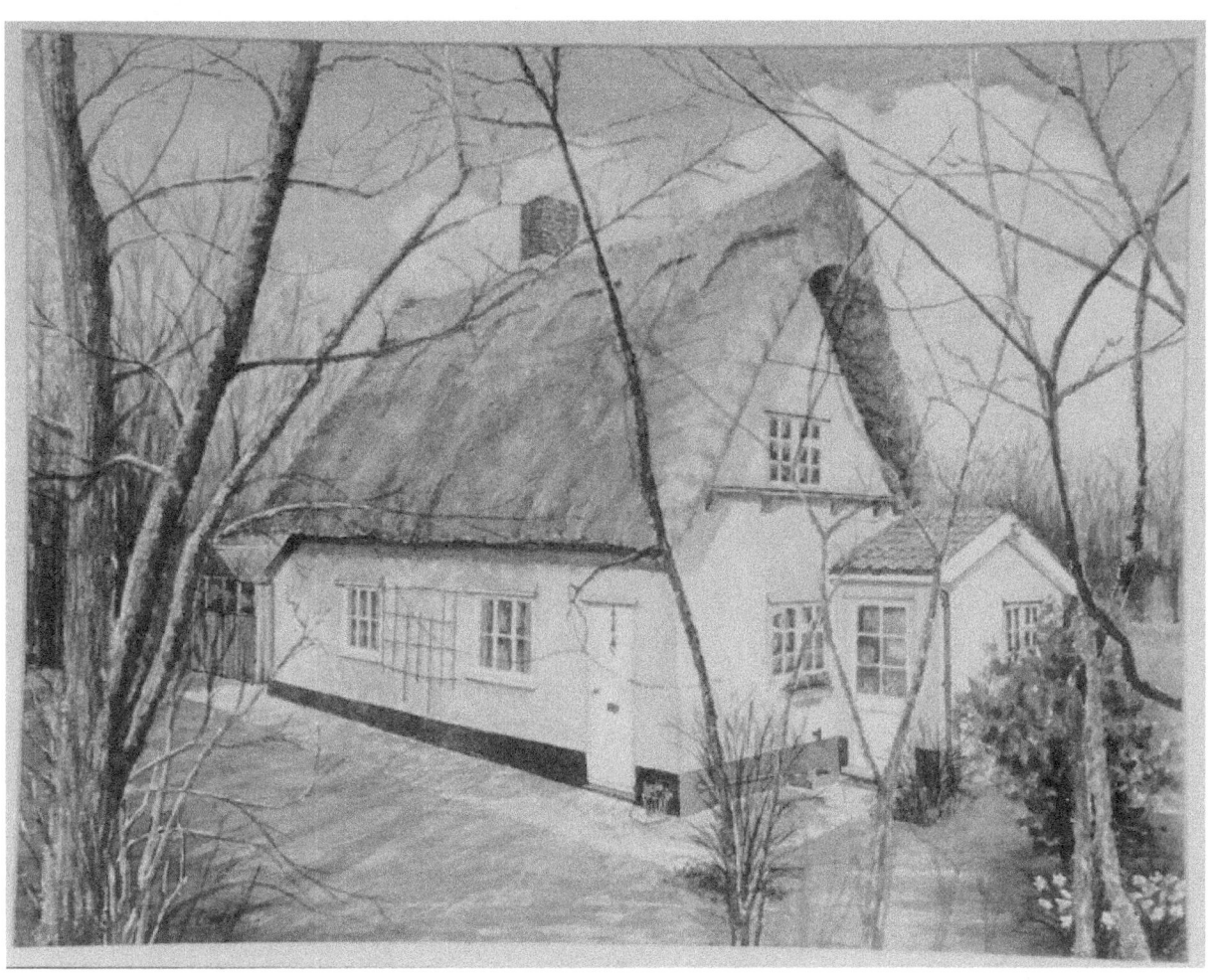

Gull Lane Cottage, 1994
m: watercolour on paper

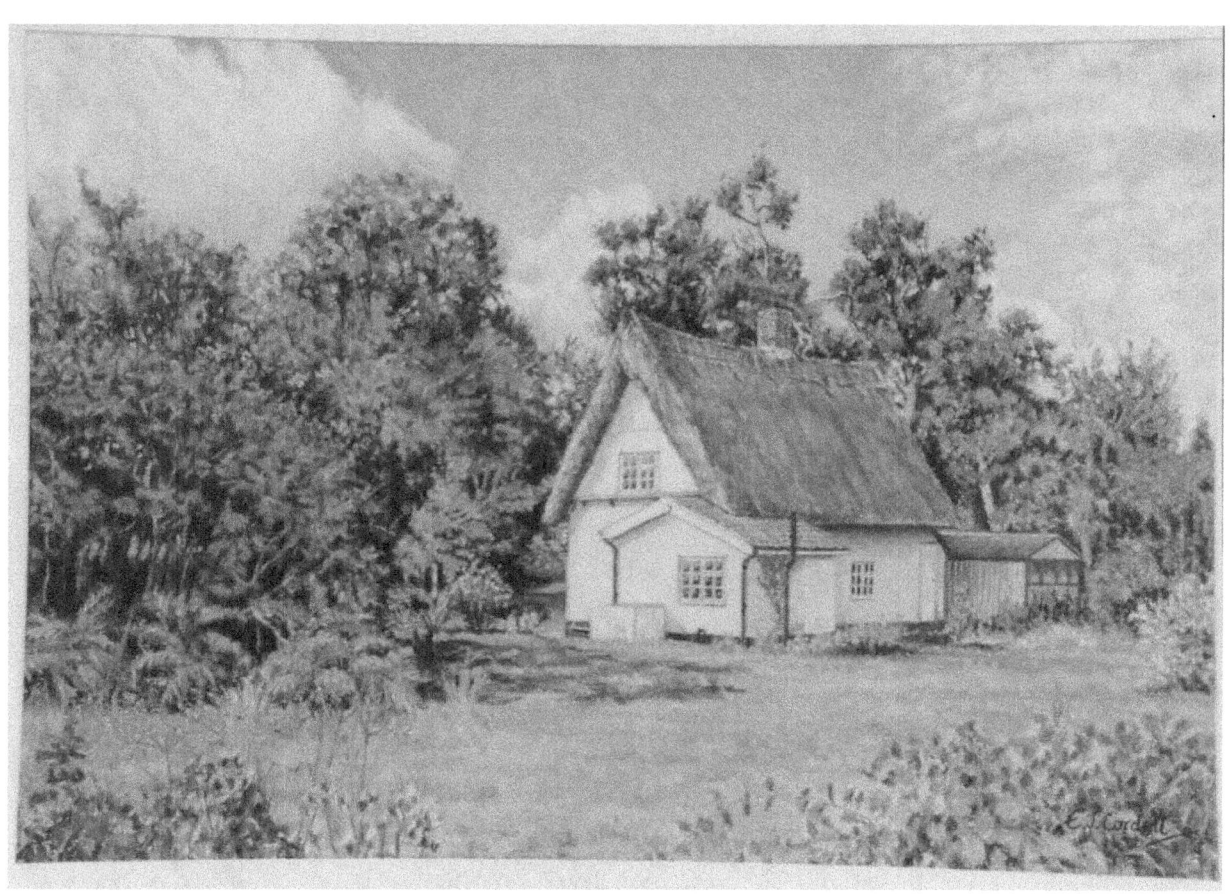

Gull Lane Cottage, 1994

m: pastel on paper

Willy Lott's cottage at Flatford Mill in Suffolk, 1994

m: pastel on paper

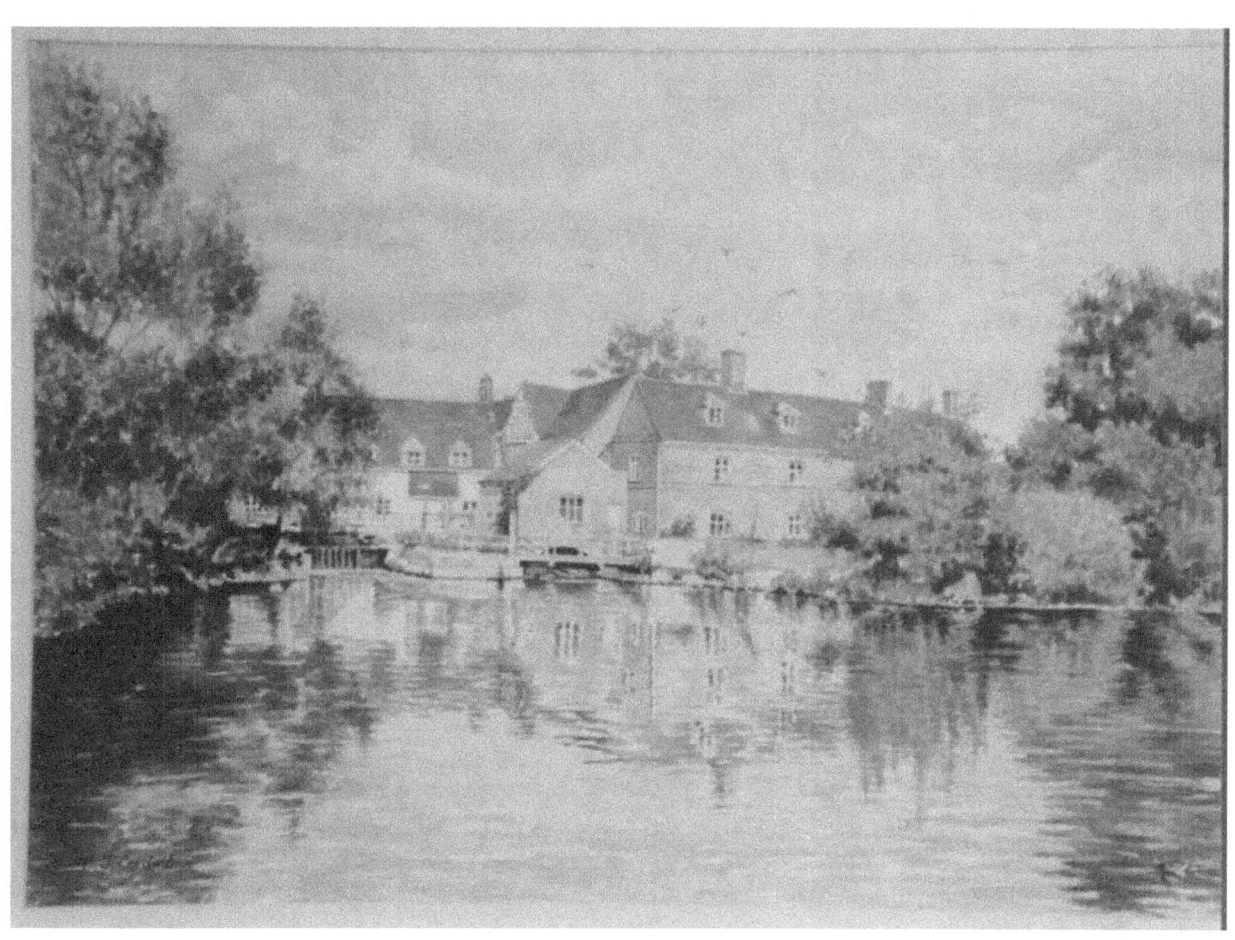

Flatford Mill in Constable country, 1994

m: pastel on paper

Wharf Cottage, 1994

m: watercolour on paper

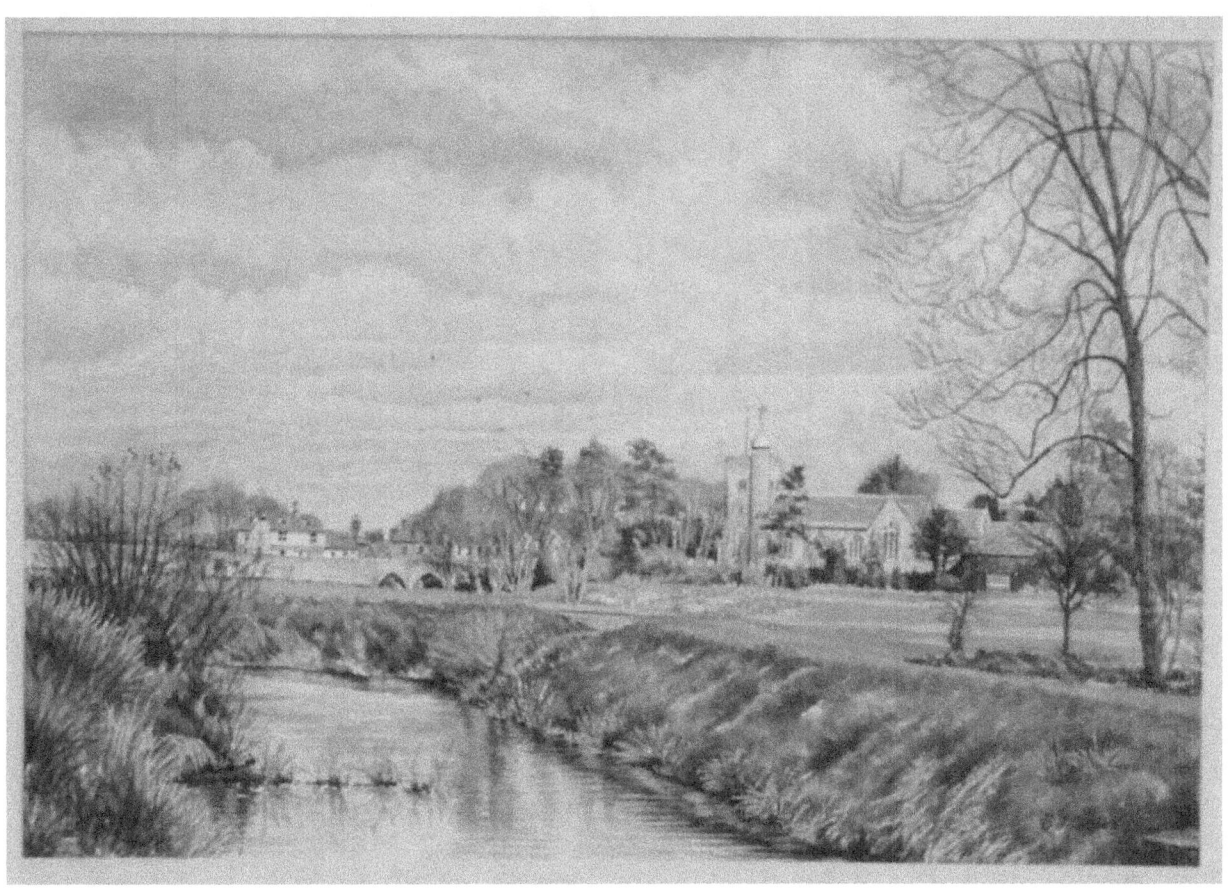

Church and bridge at Yalding in Kent, 1995

m: watercolour on paper

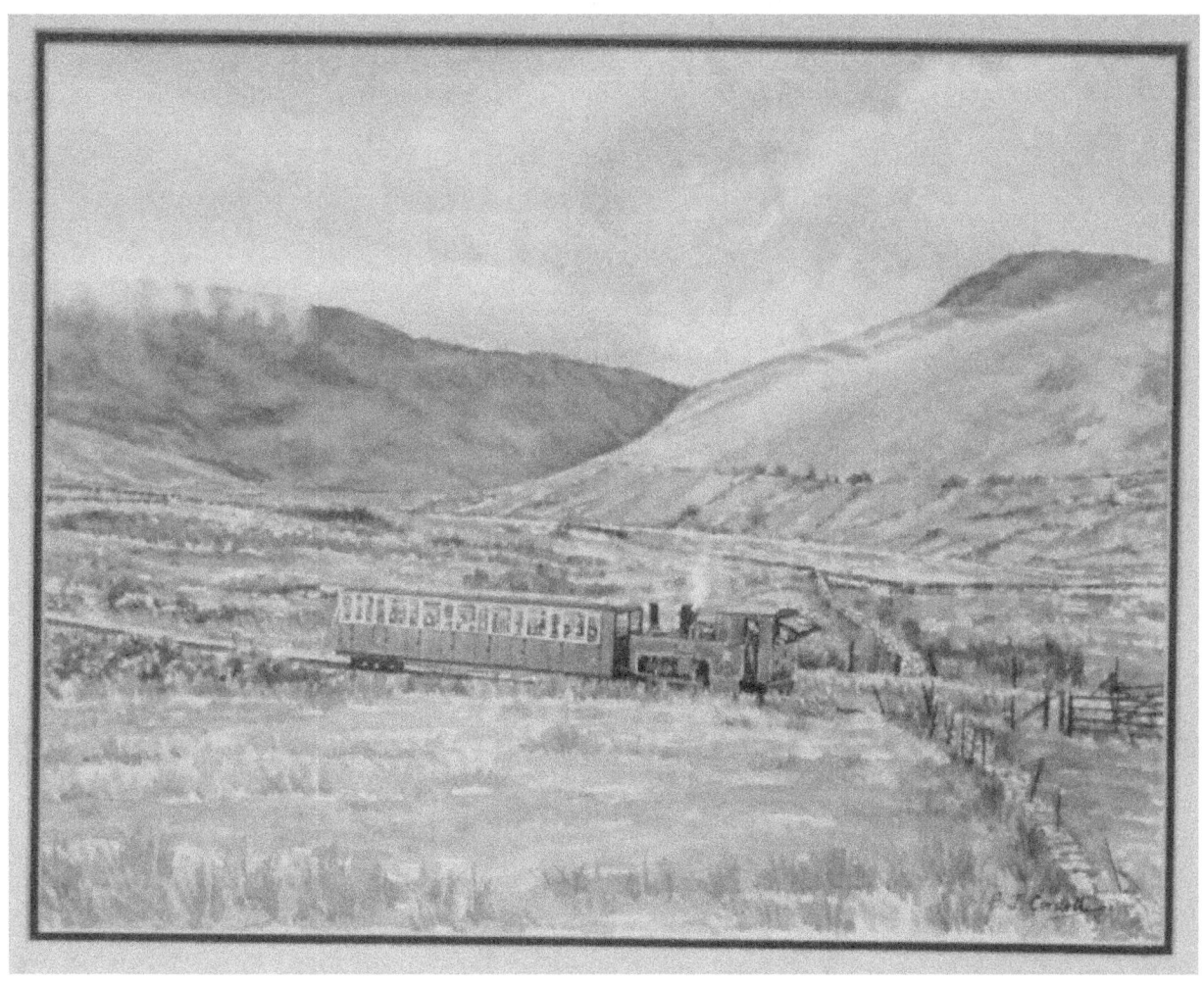

Snowdon Railway, 1997
m: watercolour on paper

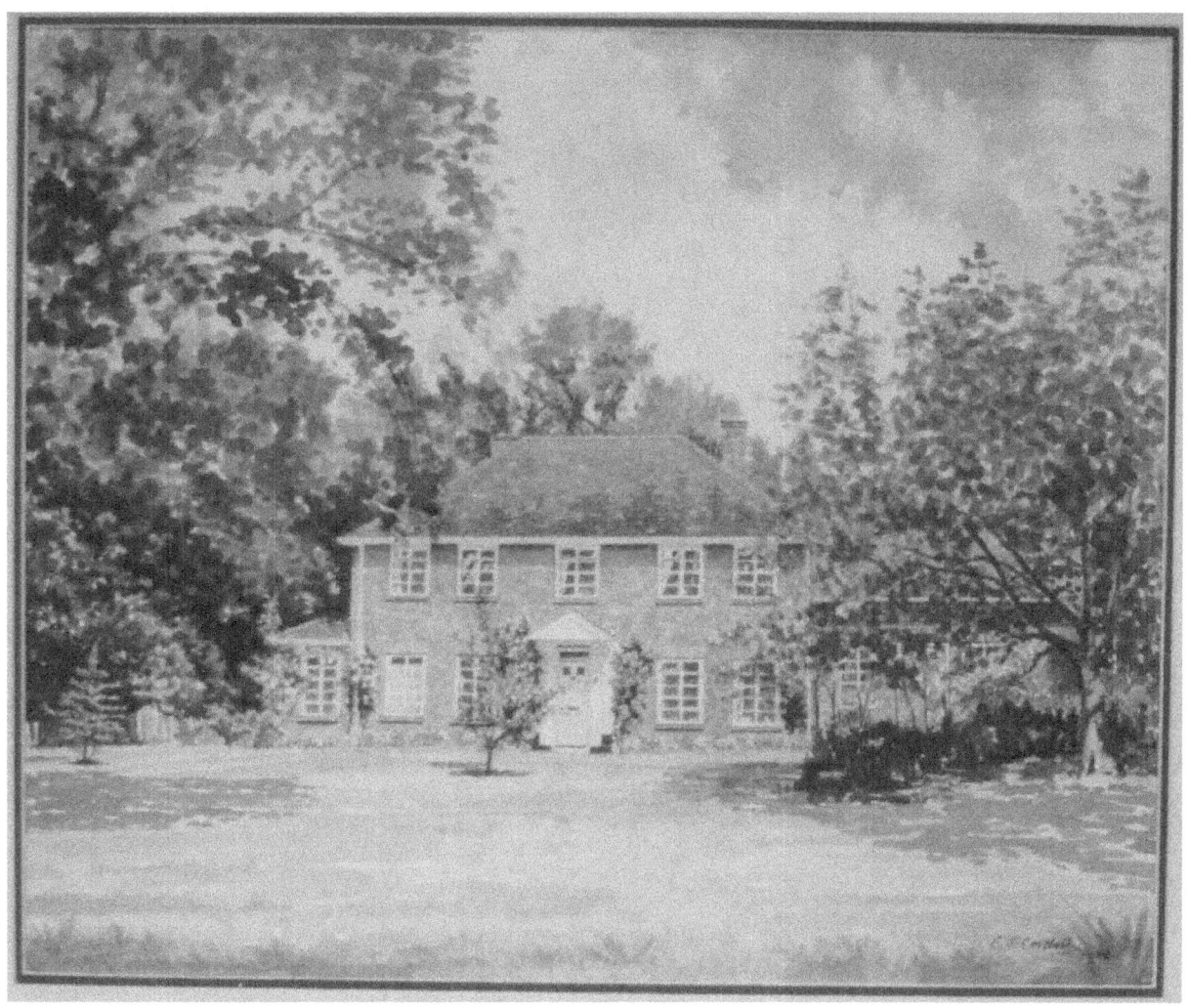

Old pump house and grounds, 1998

m: watercolour on paper

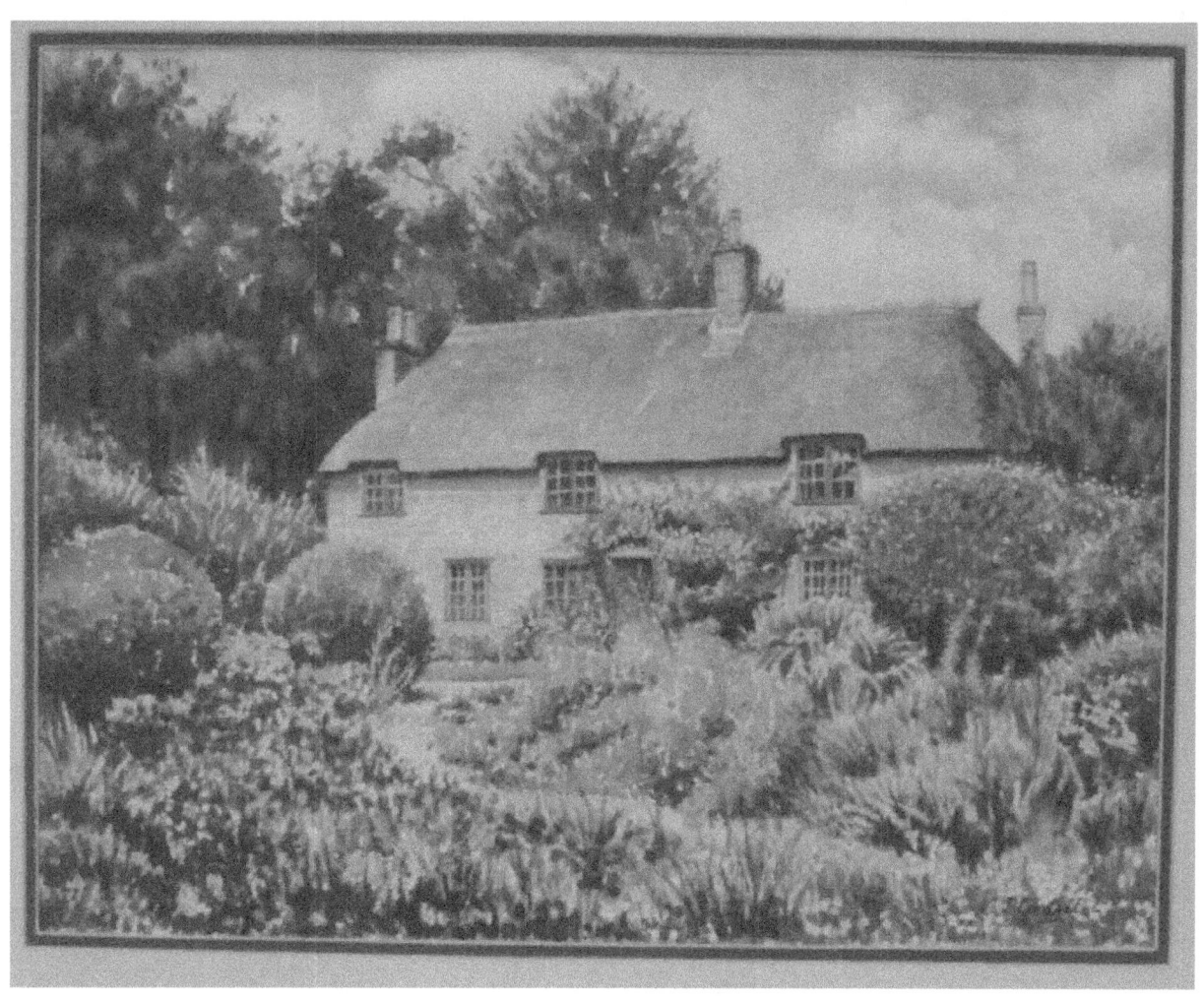

Thomas Hardy's cottage in Dorset, 2000
m: watercolour on paper

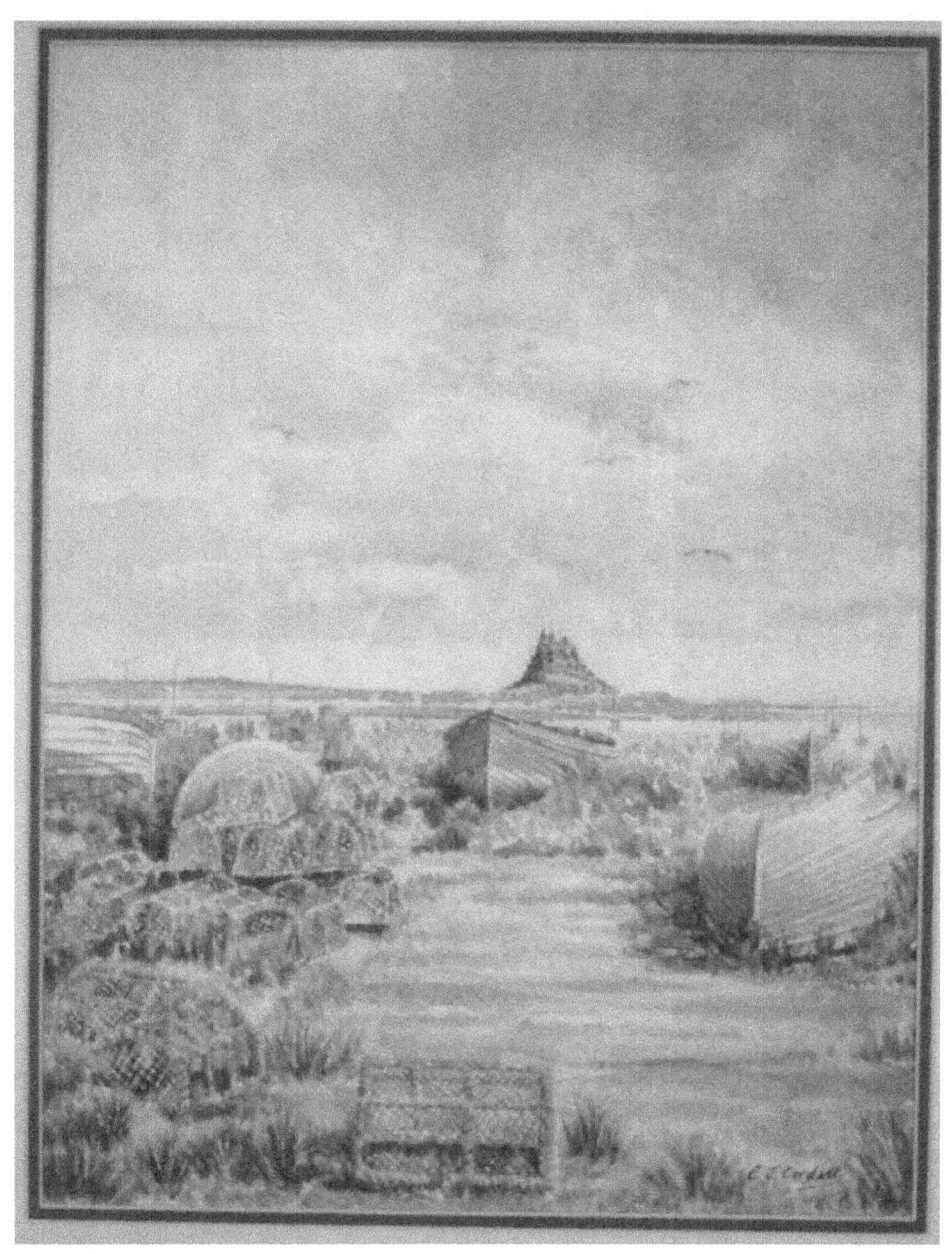

The Holy Island of Lindisfarne, 2000

m: watercolour on paper

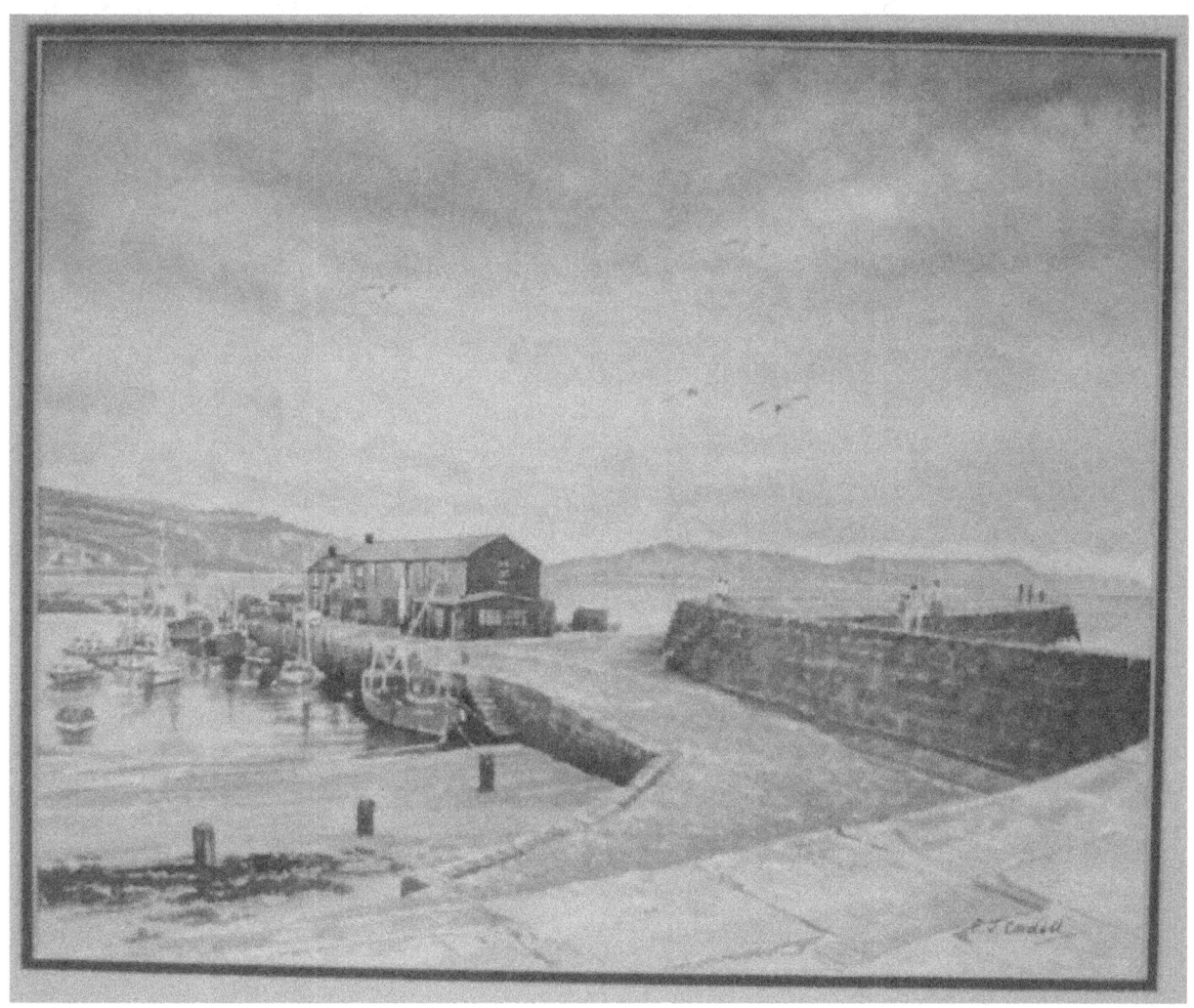

The Cobb at Lyme Regis, 2000
m: watercolour on paper

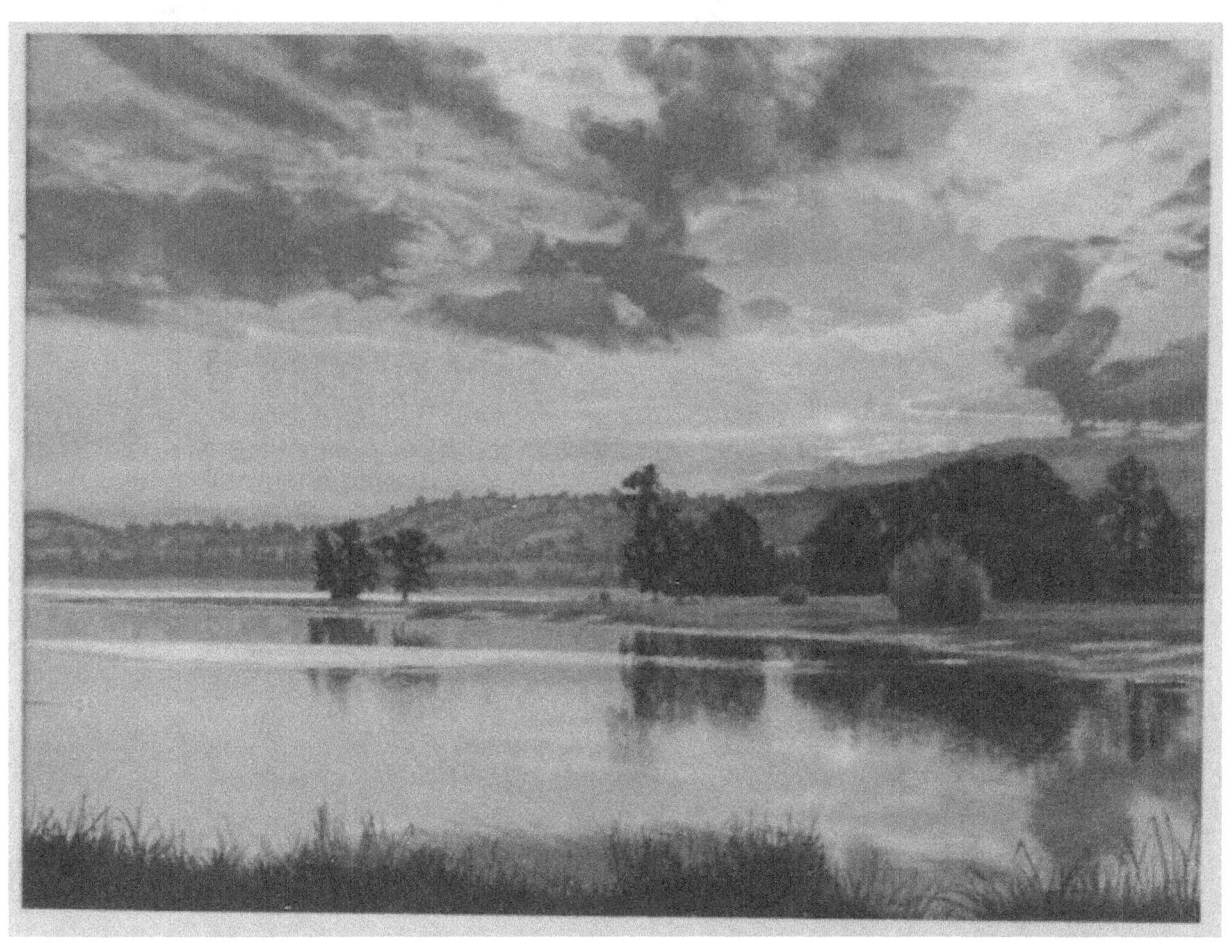

Sunset on the Rye marshes, 2003

m: pastel on paper

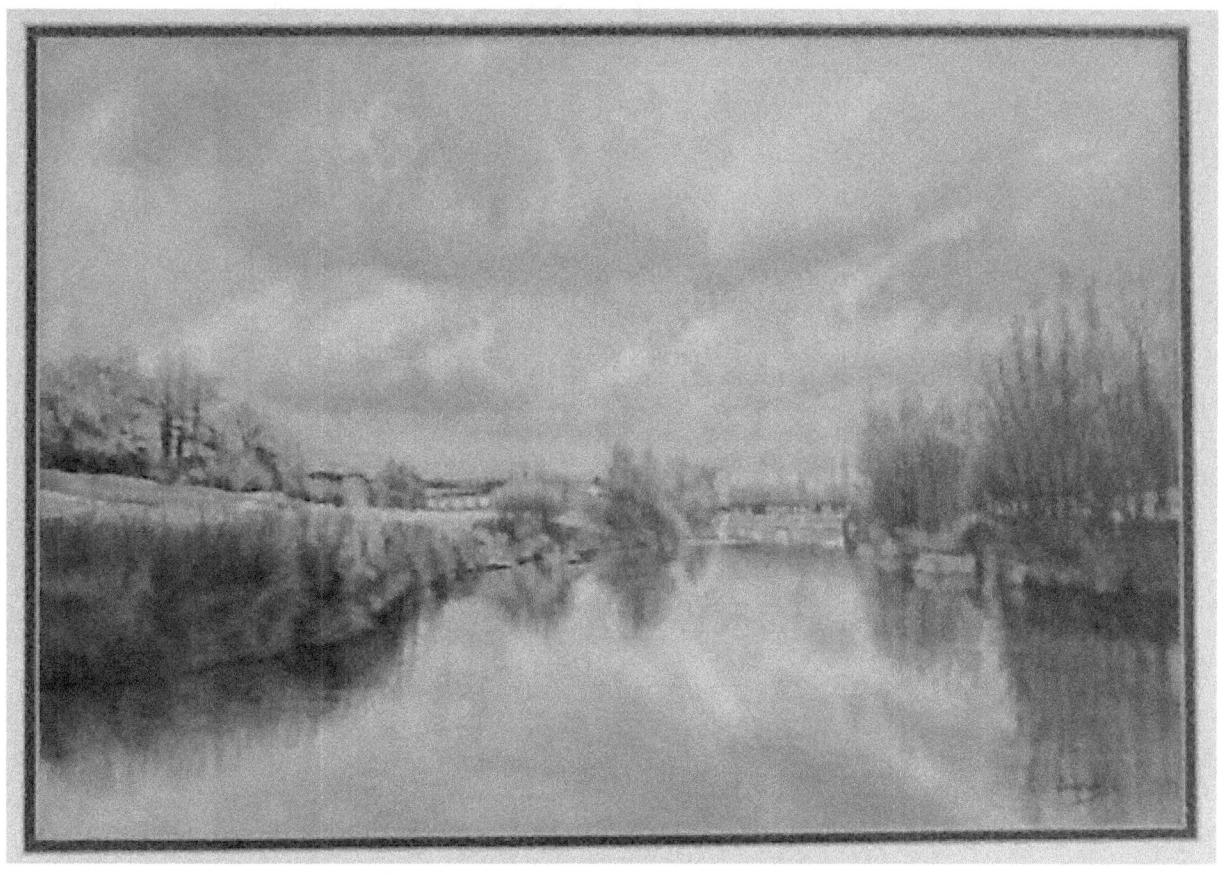

The river Medway near Yalding, 2003

m: pastel on paper

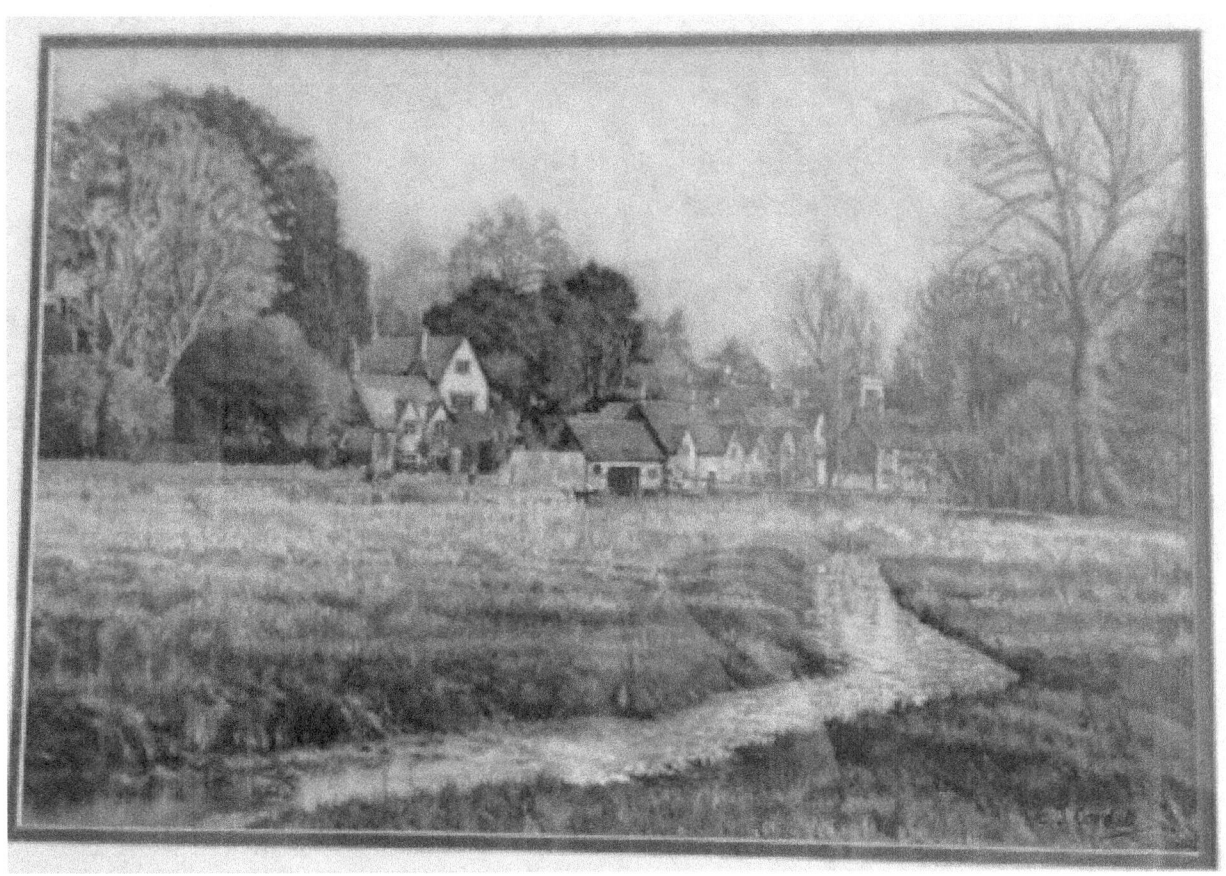

The Cotswolds village of Blbury, 2008
m: pastel on paper

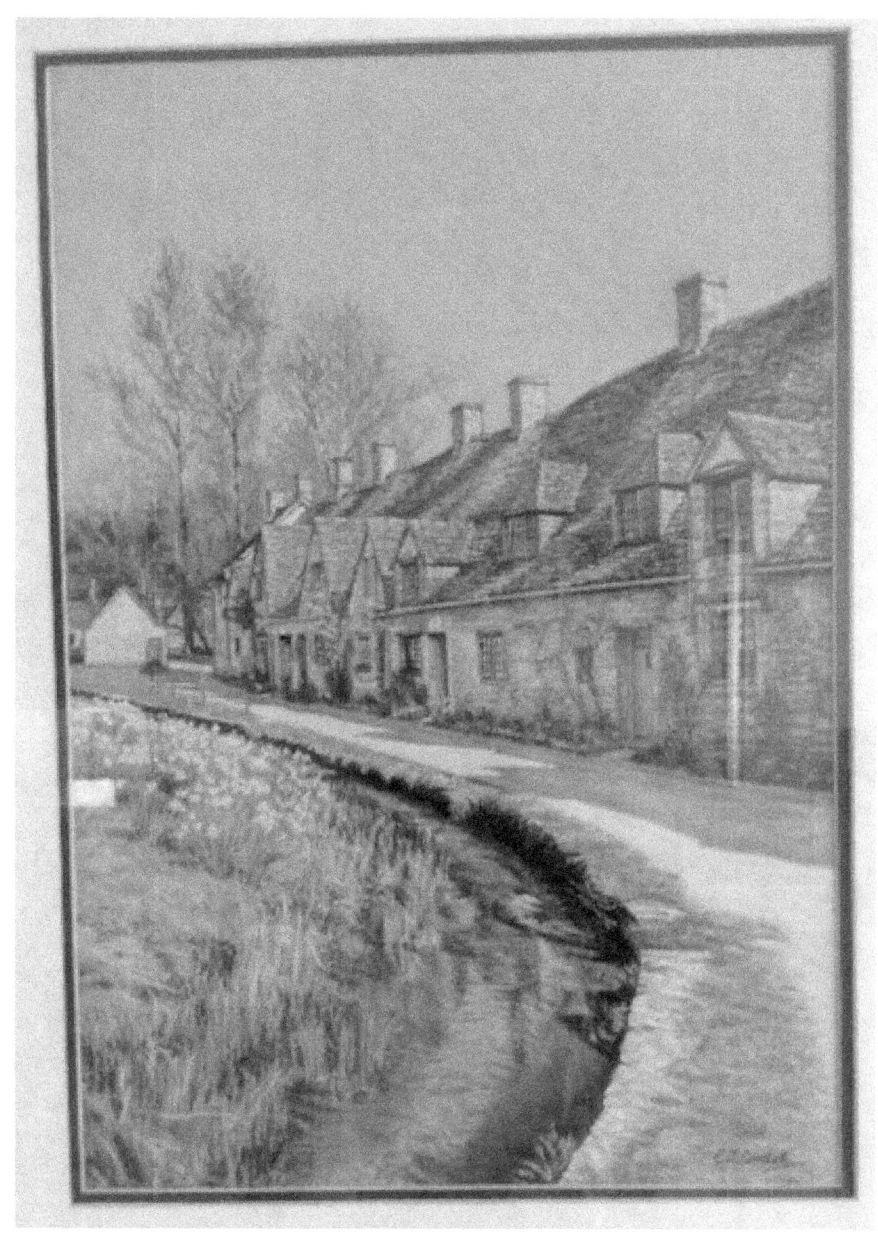

Arlington Row in the Cotswold village of Bibury, 2008

m: pastel on paper

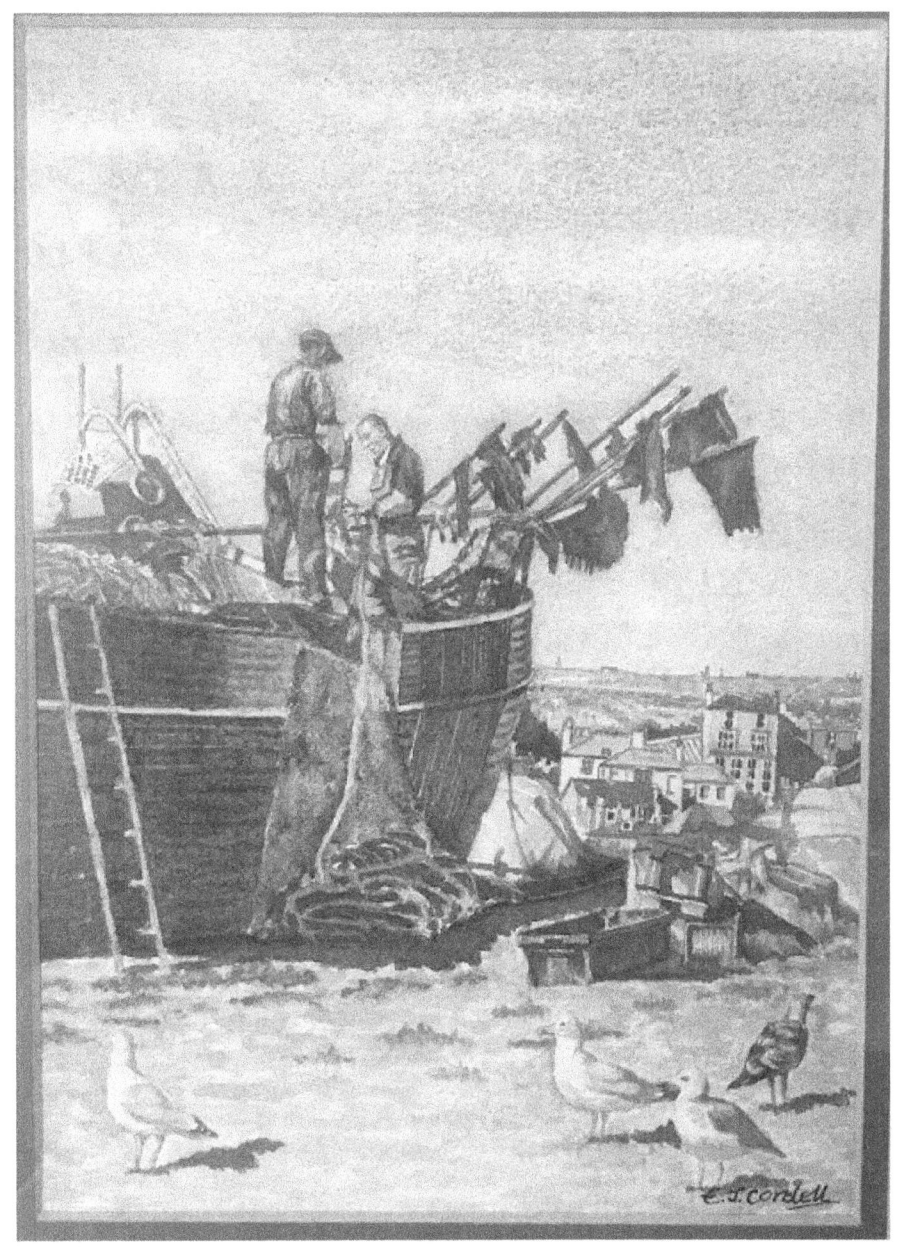

Fishermen at Hastings, date unknown

m: watercolour on paper

2 PORTRAITS

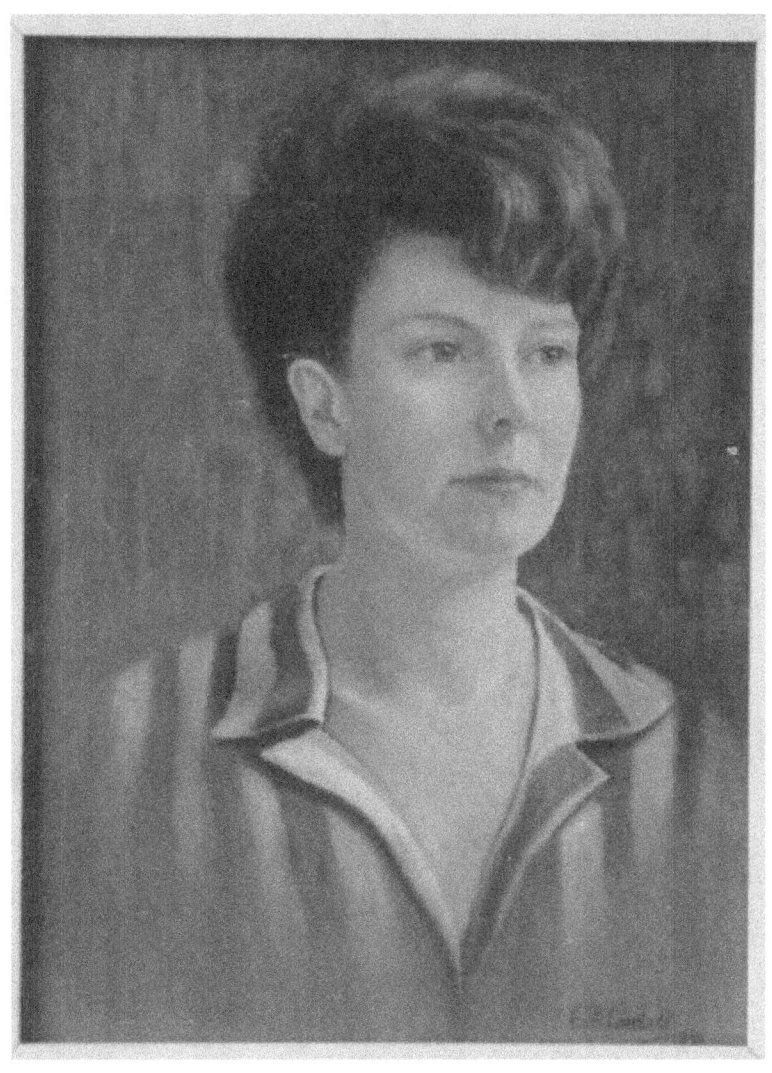

Eileen, 1975

m: pastel on paper

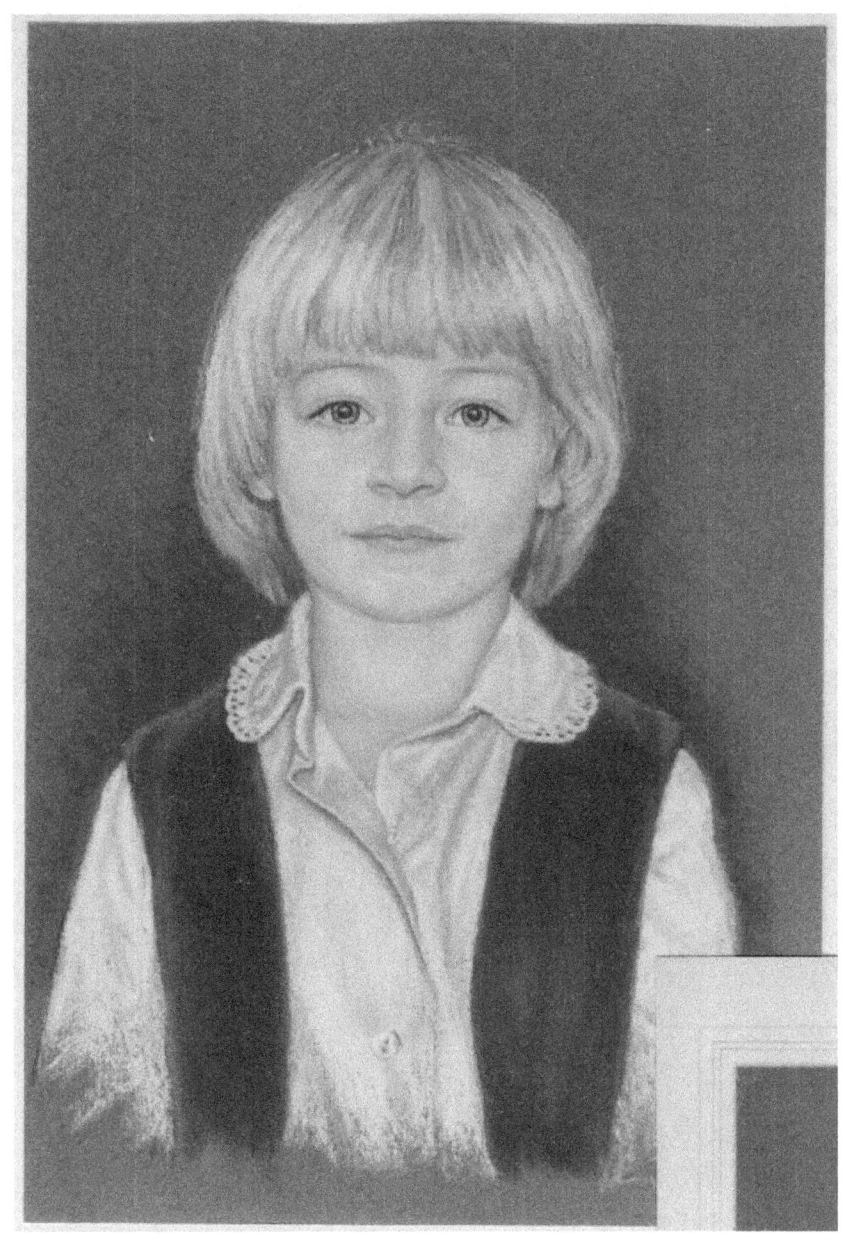

Carly, 1981
m: pastel on paper

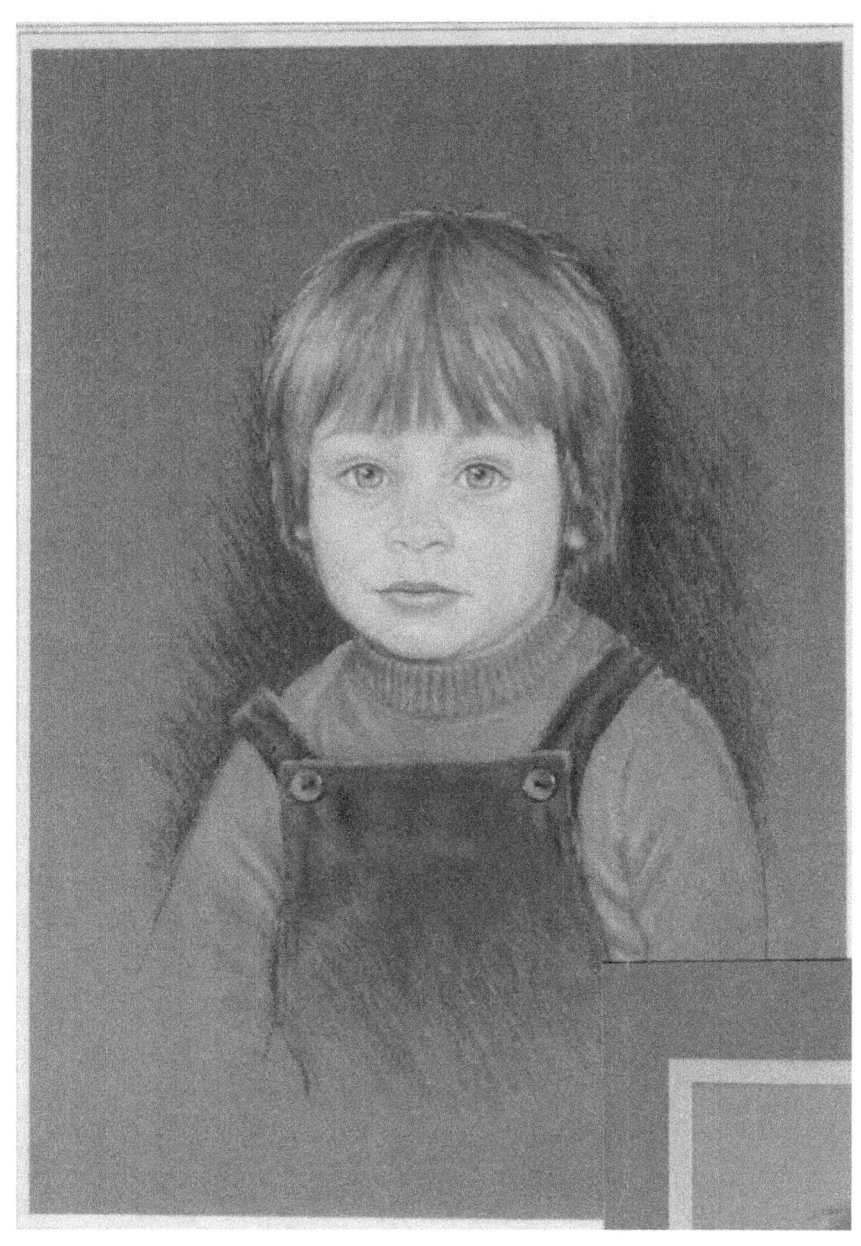

Nicholas, 1981
m: pastel on paper

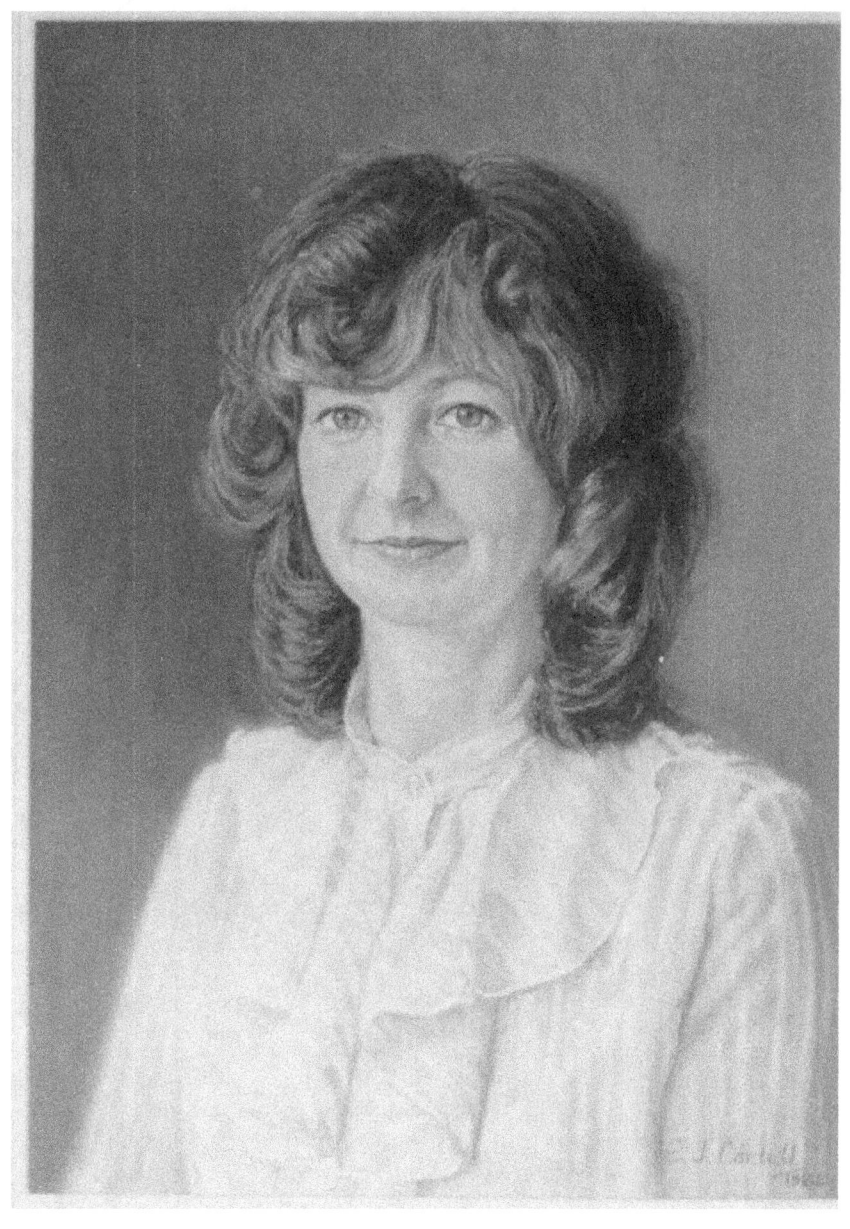

Gillian, 1982
m: pastel on paper

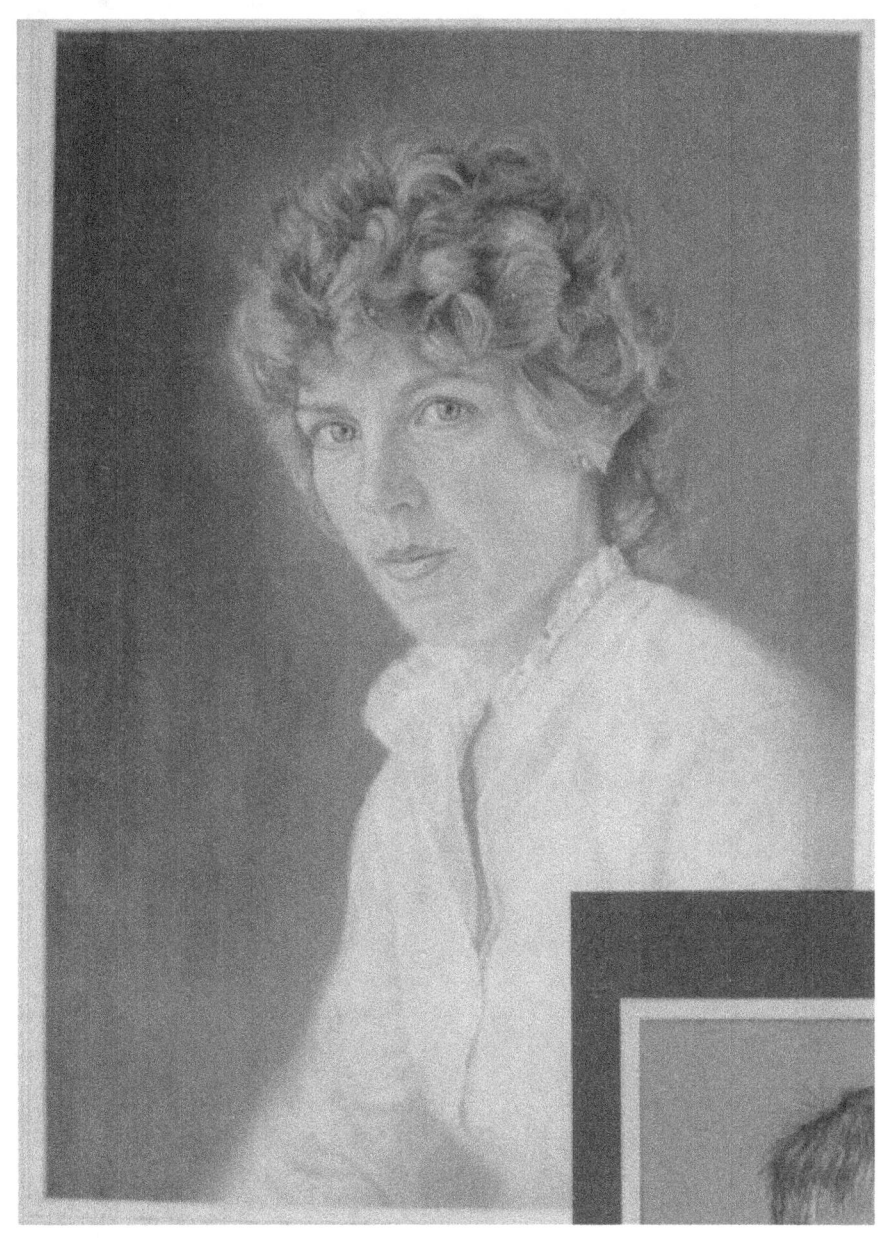

Irene, 1983
m: pastel on paper

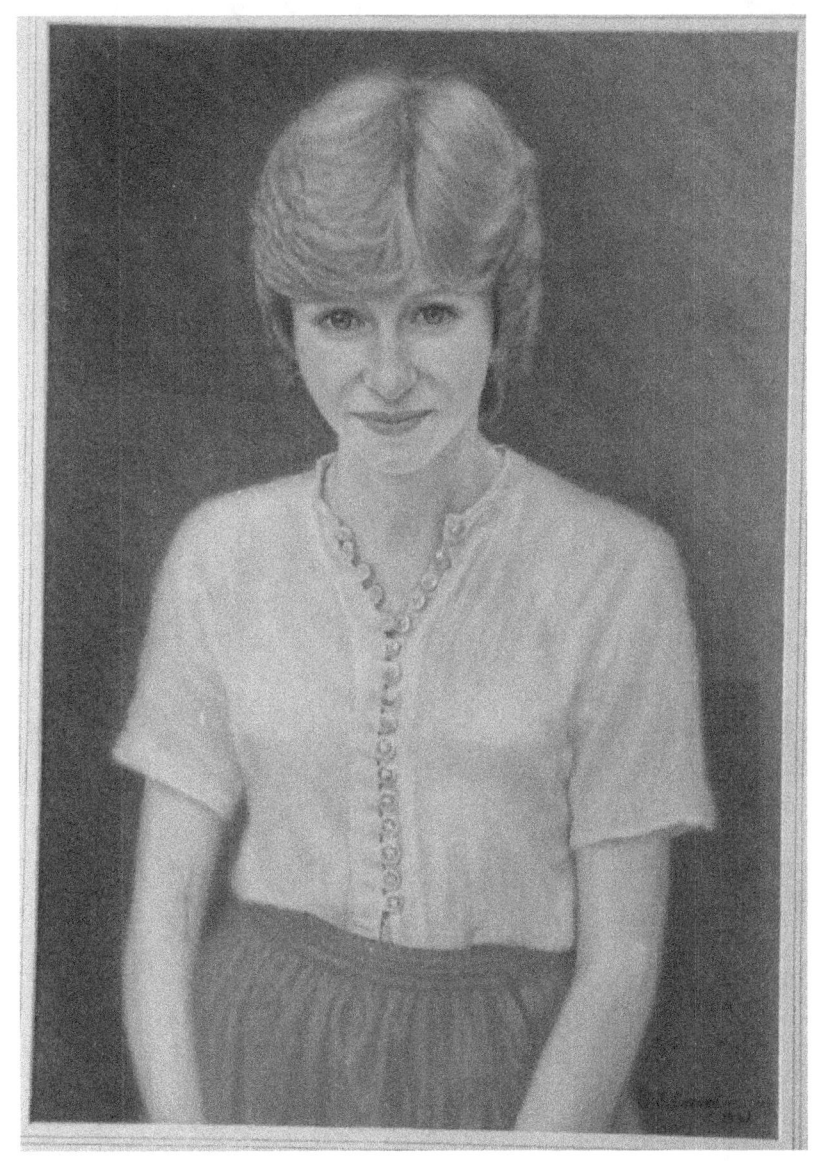

Lisa, 1984

m: pastel on paper

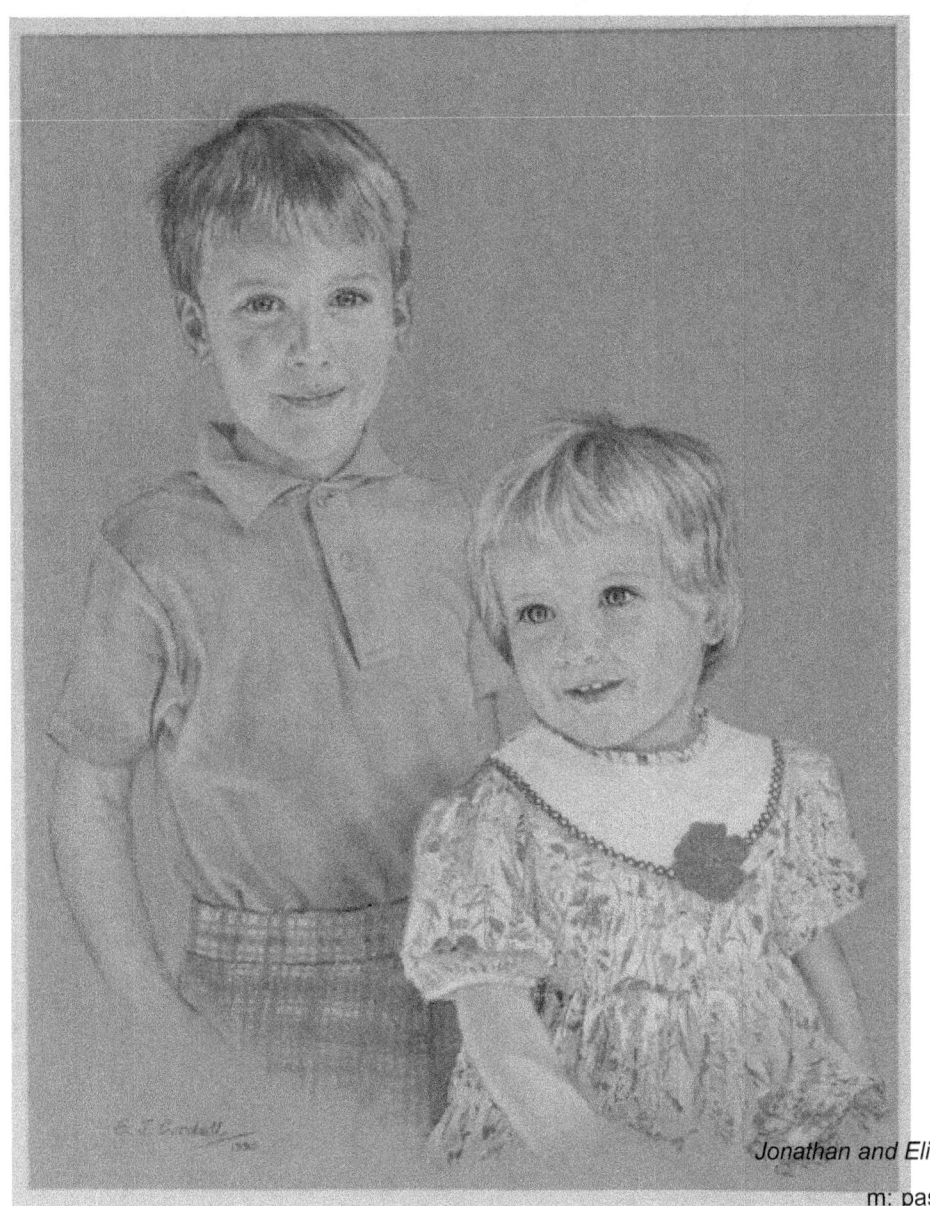

Jonathan and Elizabeth, 1990

m: pastel on paper

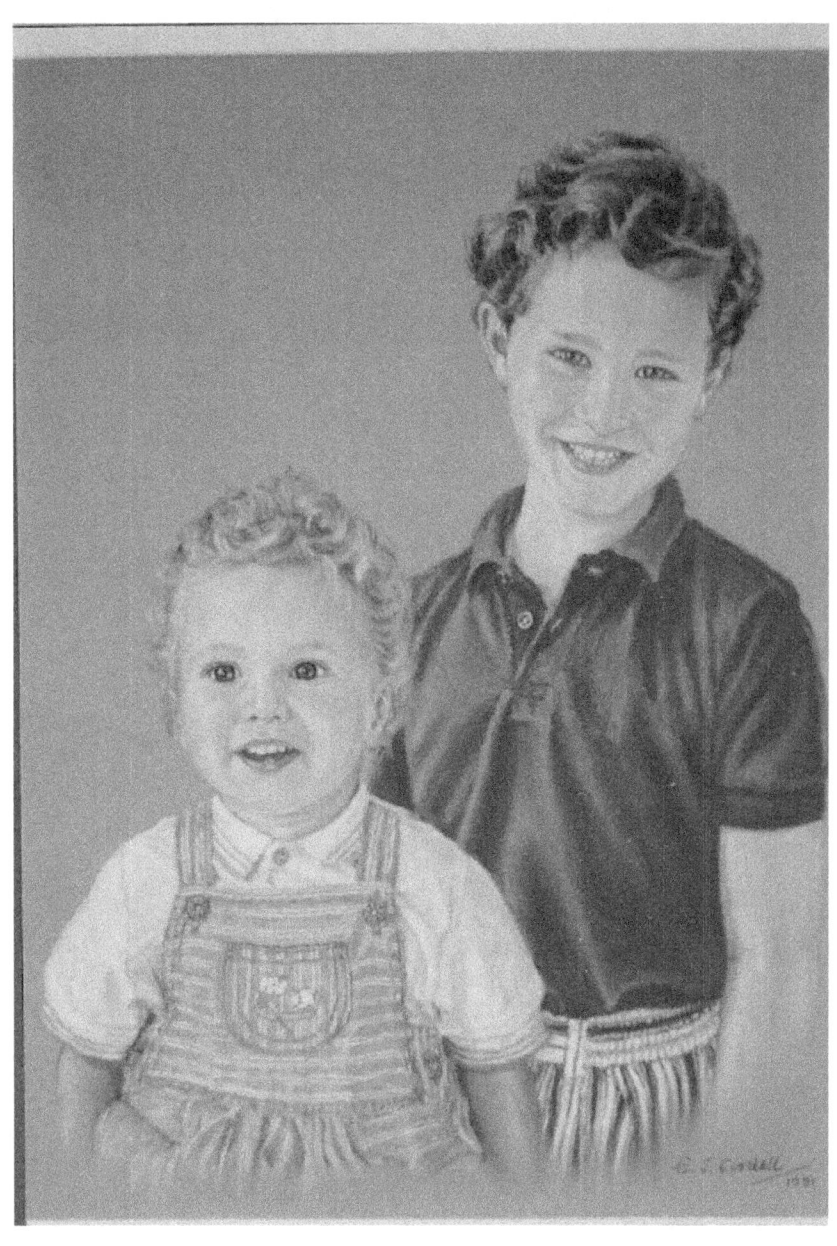

Benjamin and Dominic, 1991

m: pastel on paper

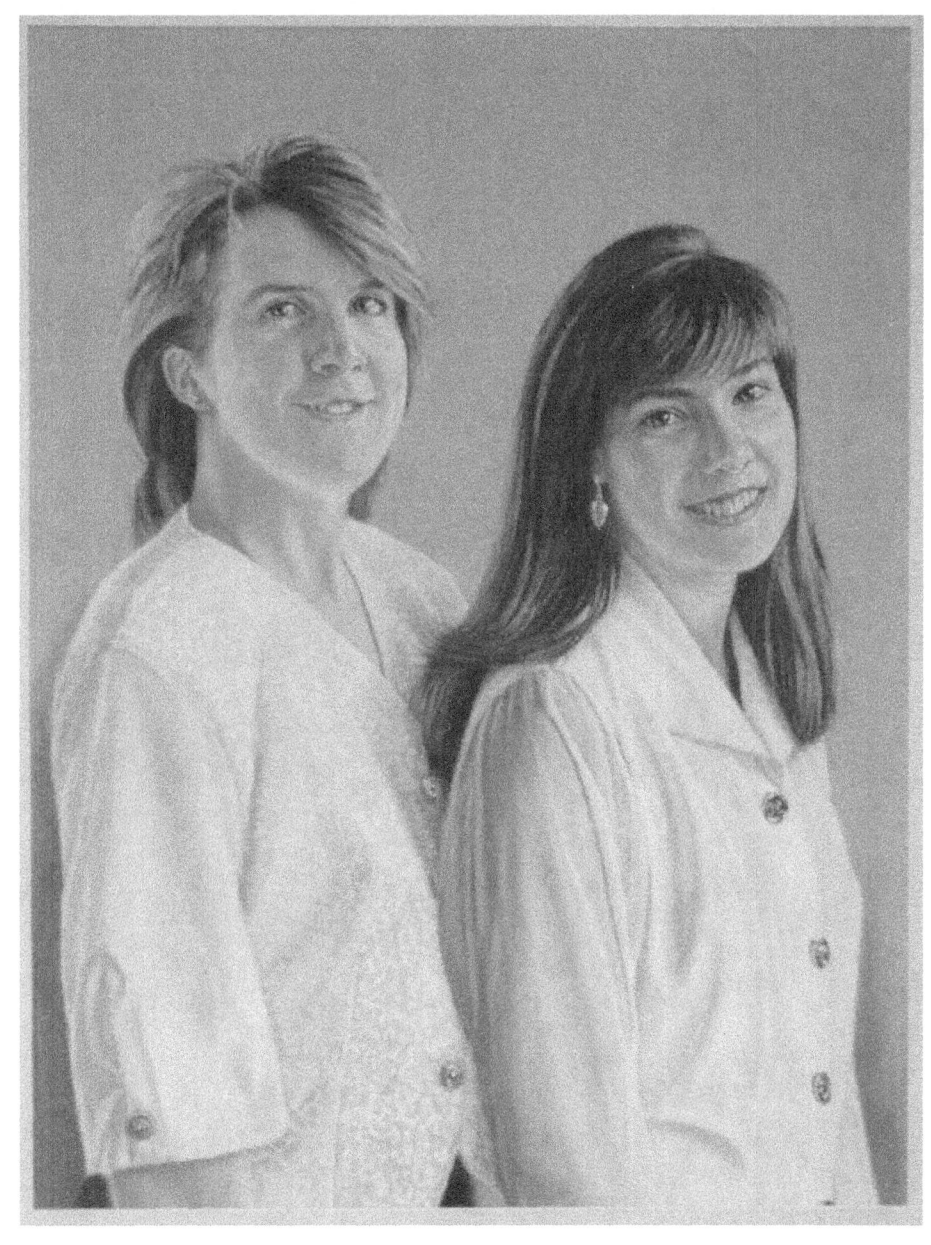

Francesca and Kerrianne, 1992
m: pastel on paper

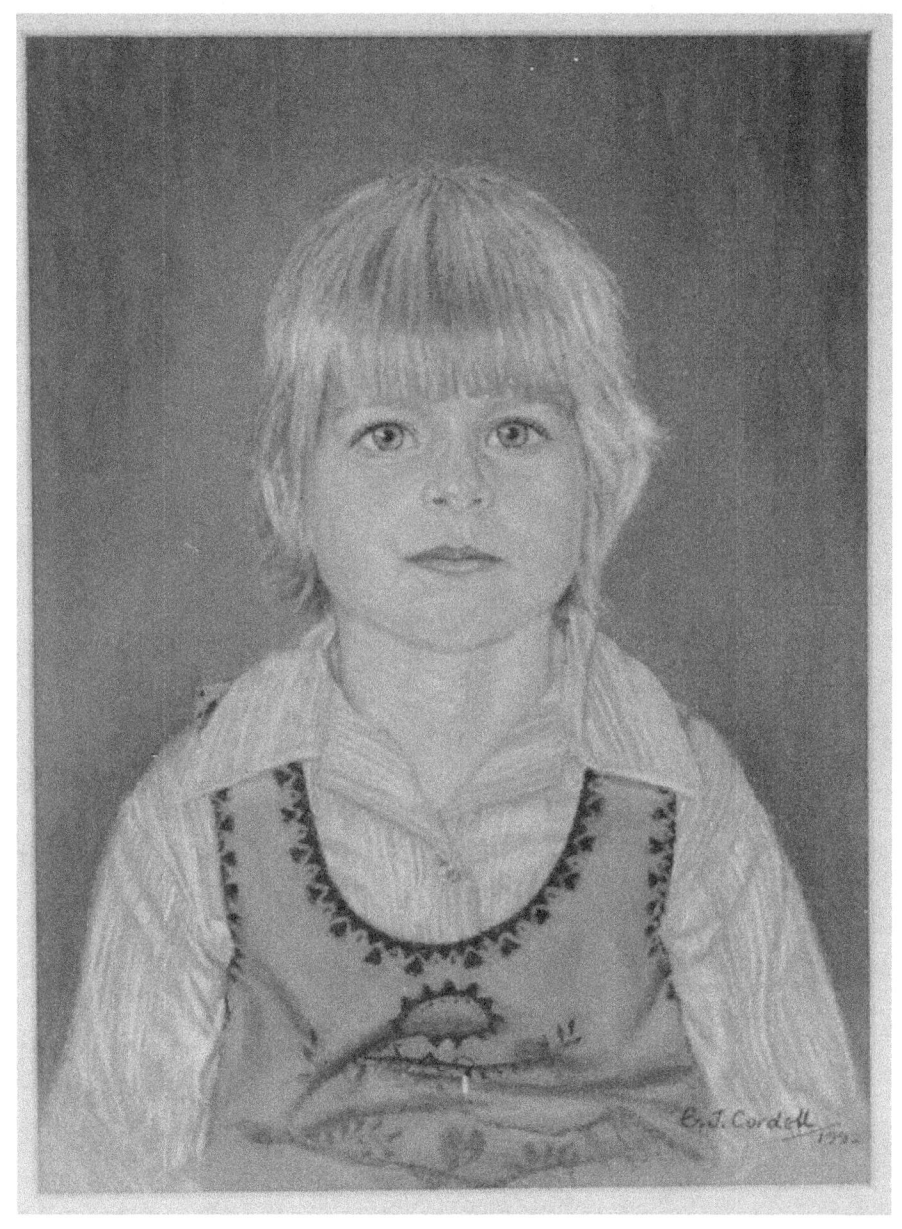

Lucy, 1992

m: pastel on paper

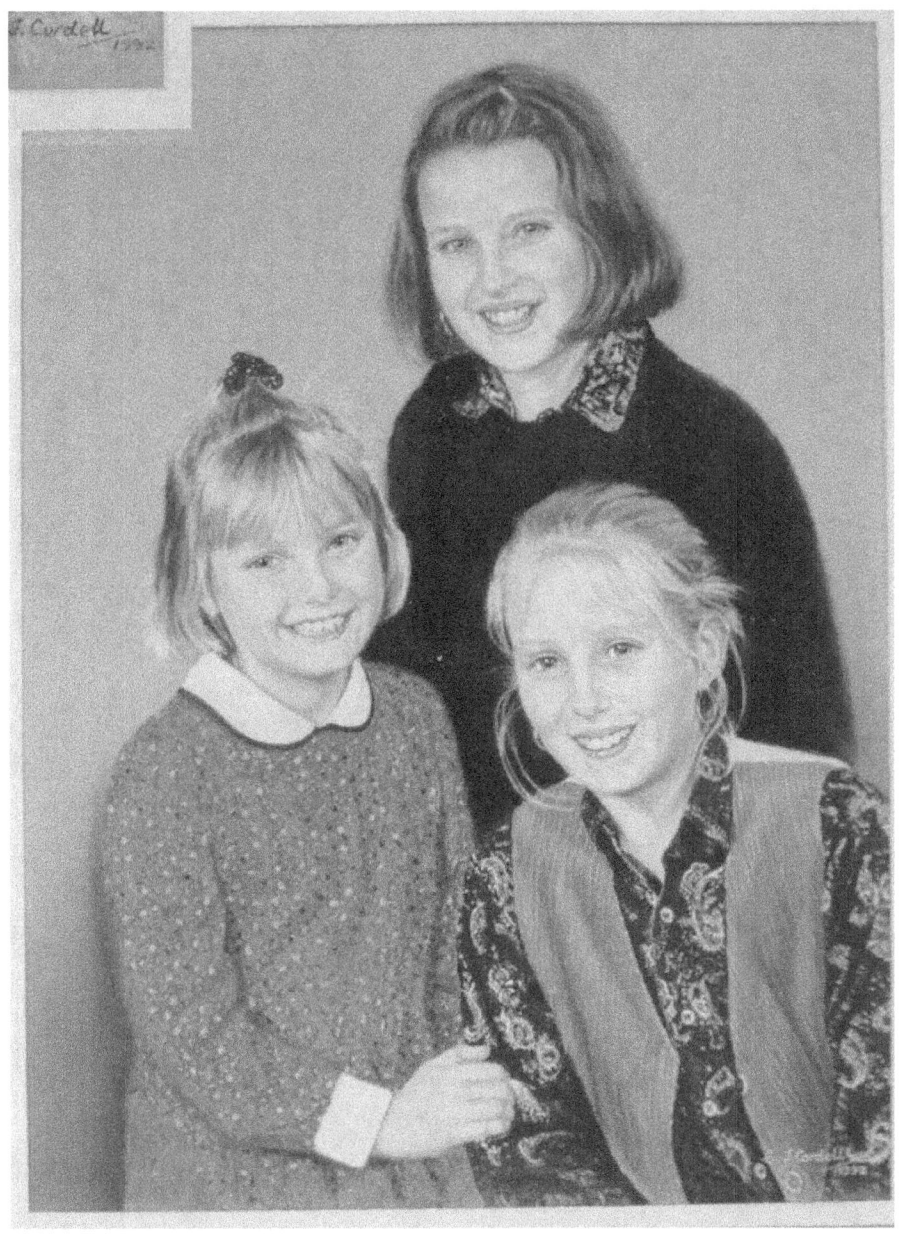

Sarah, Anna and Gemma, 1992

m: pastel on paper

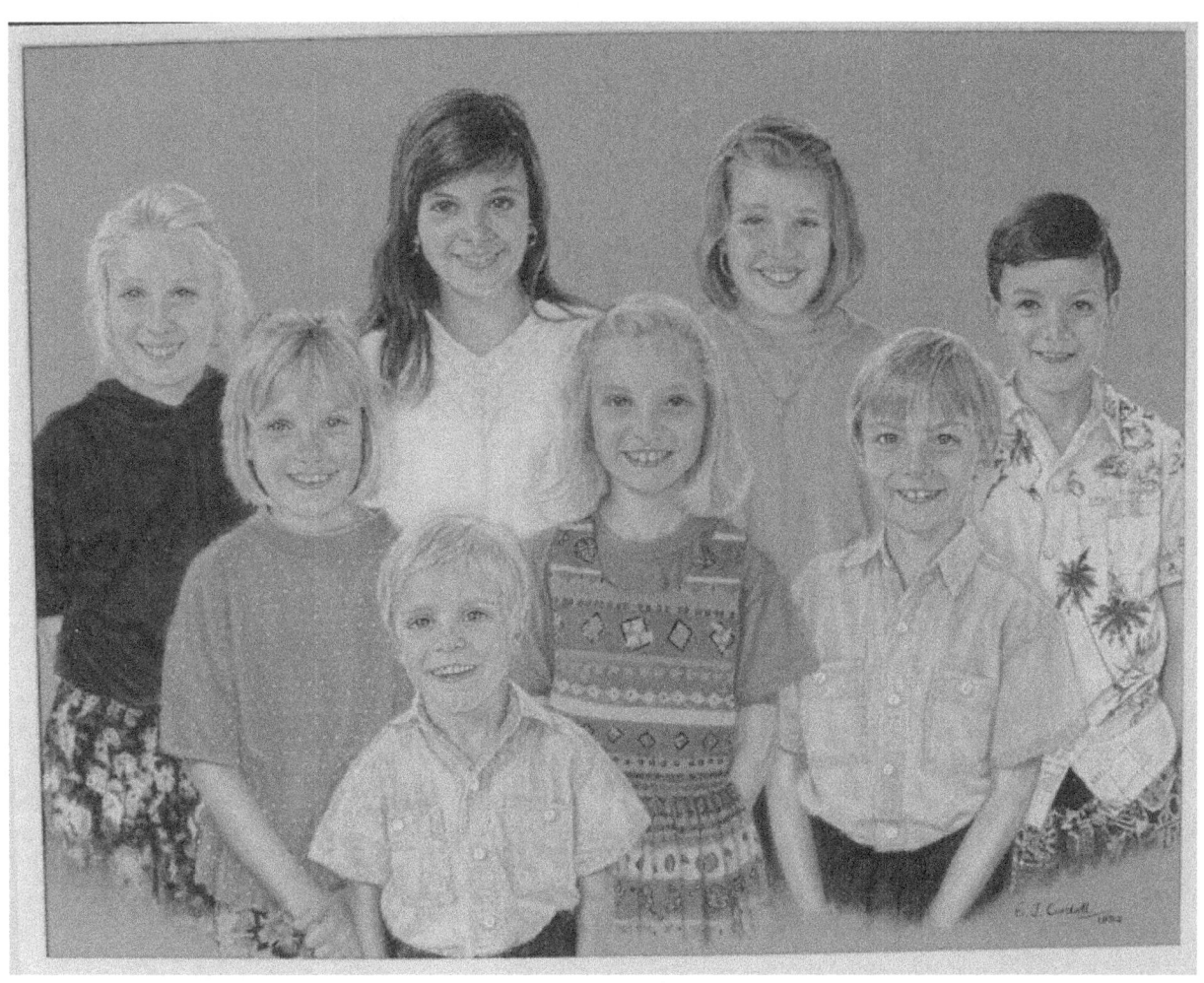

Grandchildren, 1992
m: pastel on paper

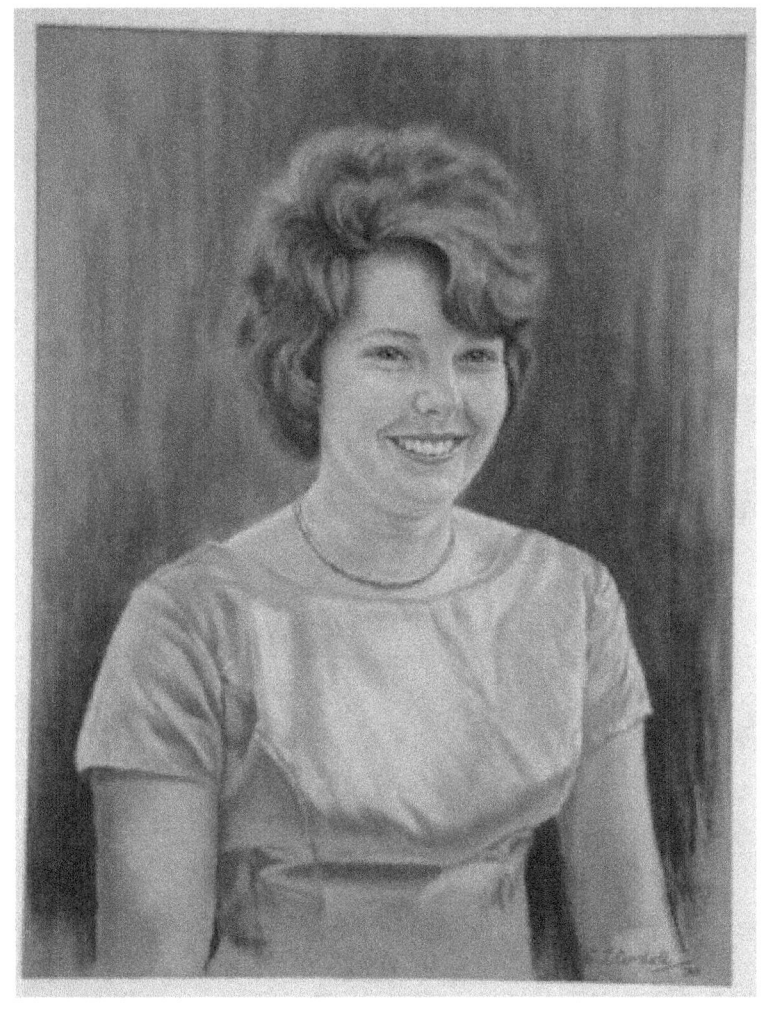

Eileen, 1993

m: pastel on paper

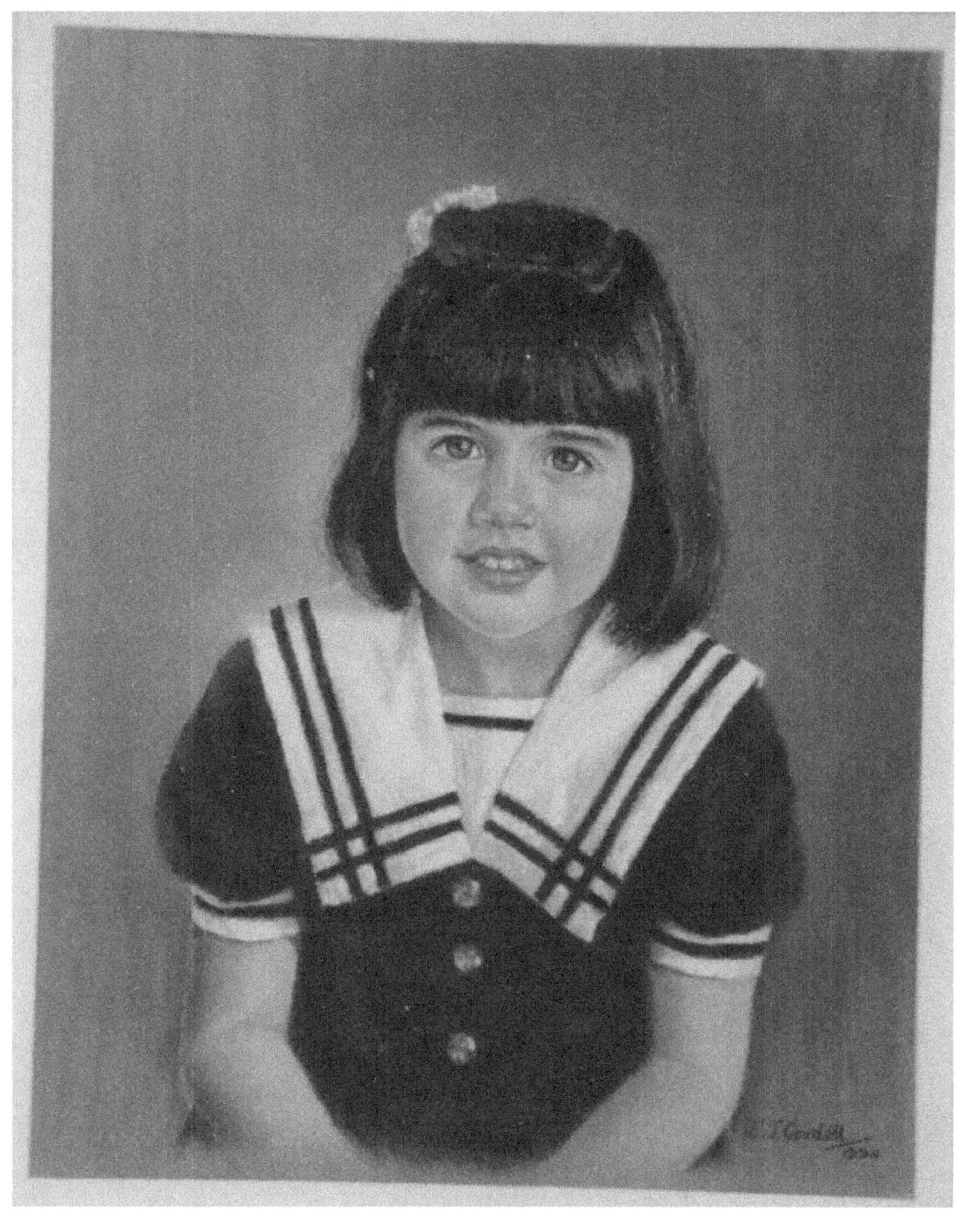

Young Girl, 1994
m: pastel on paper

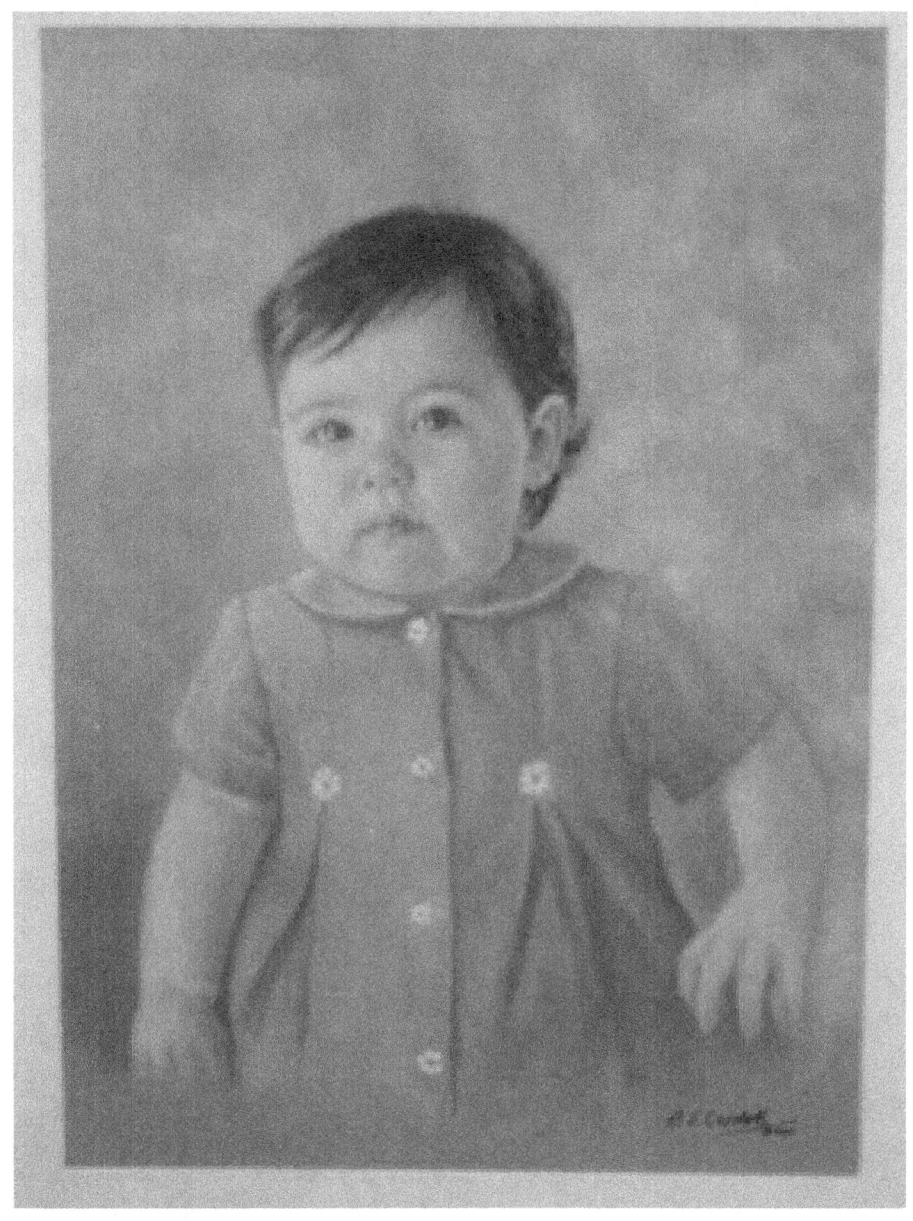

Baby girl, 2001
m: watercolour on paper

3 PETS

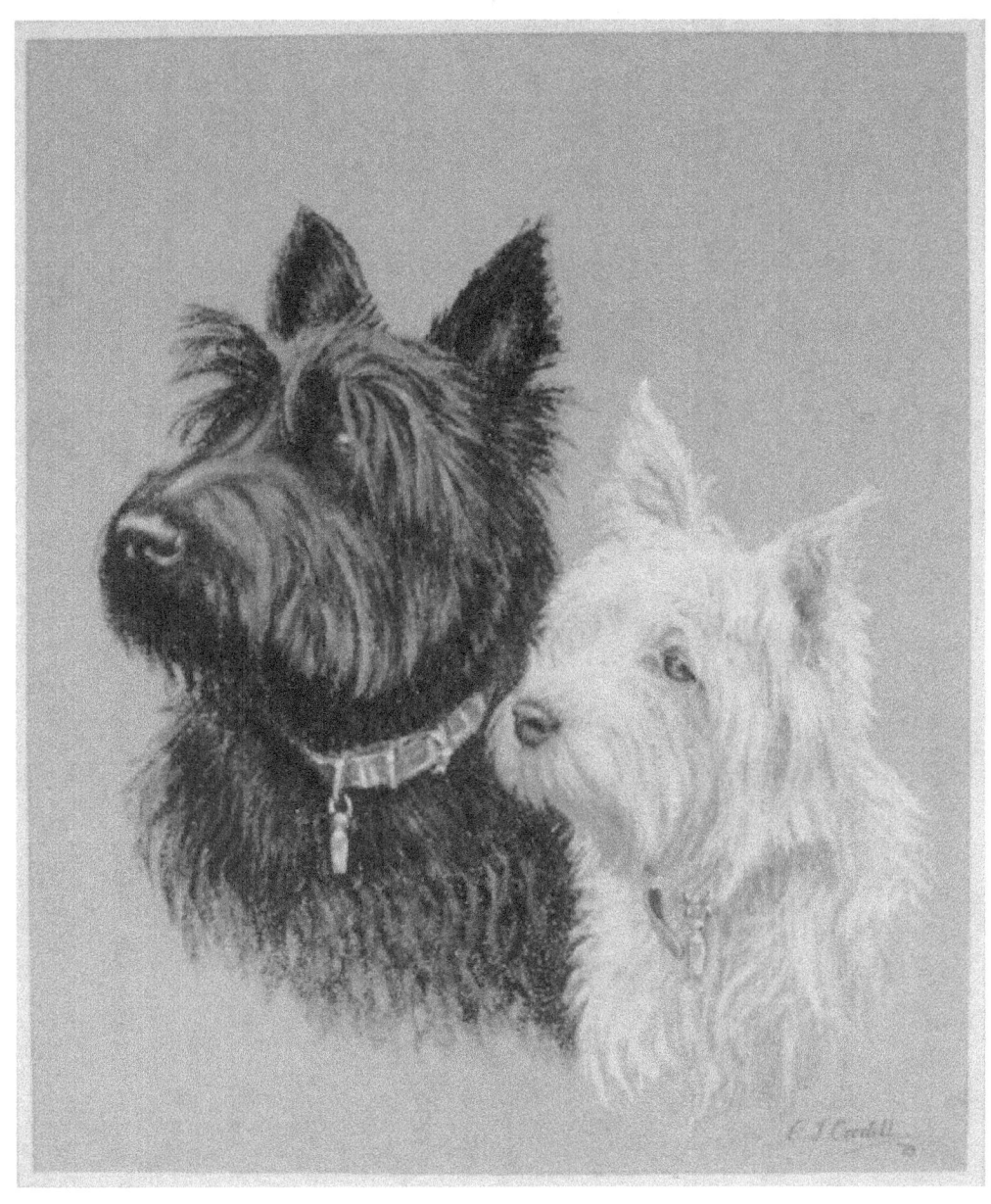

Scottie and Westie 1979

m: pastel on paper

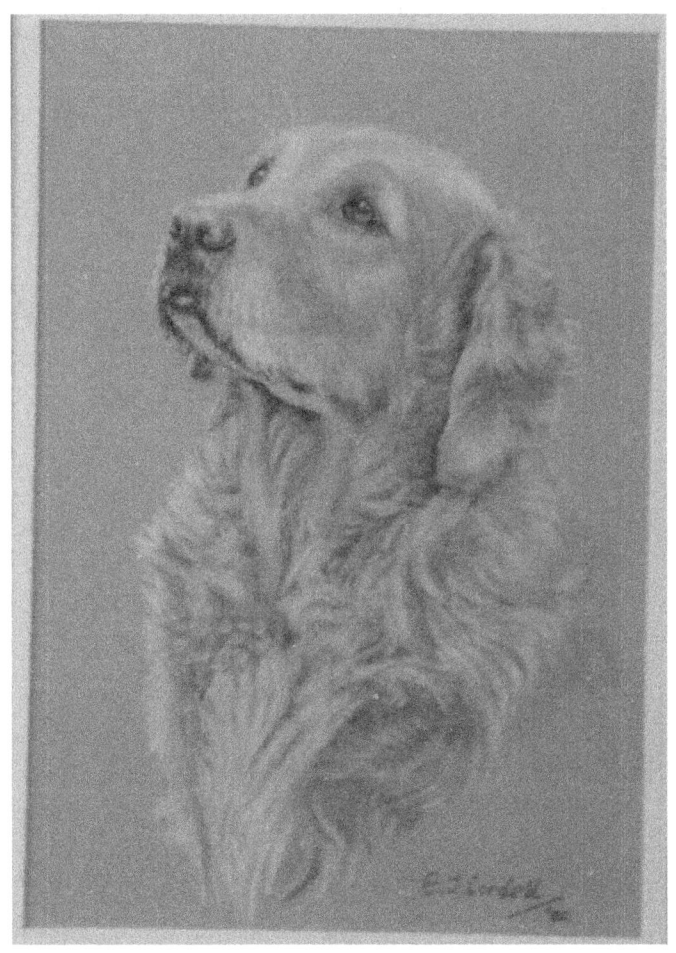

Golden Retriever, 1980

m: pastel on paper

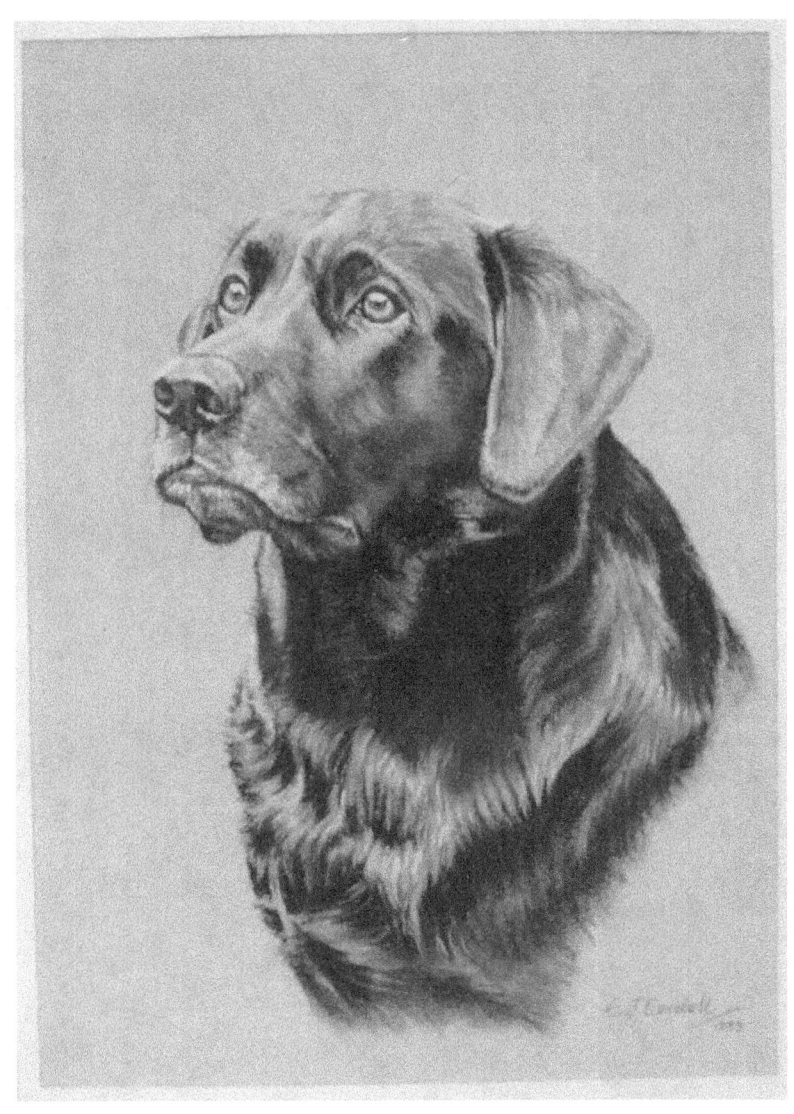

Black Labrador, 1985

m: pastel on paper

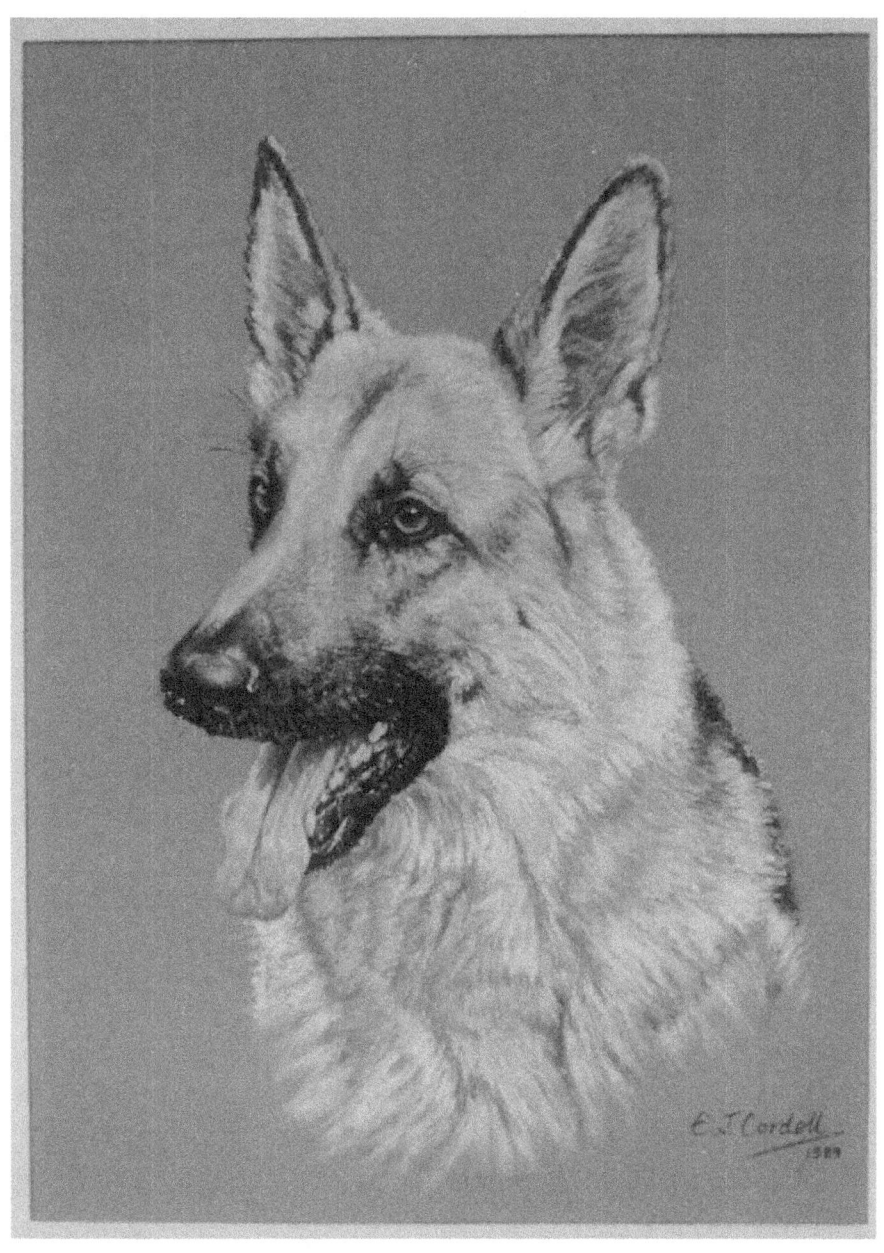

Alsatian, 1989

m: pastel on paper

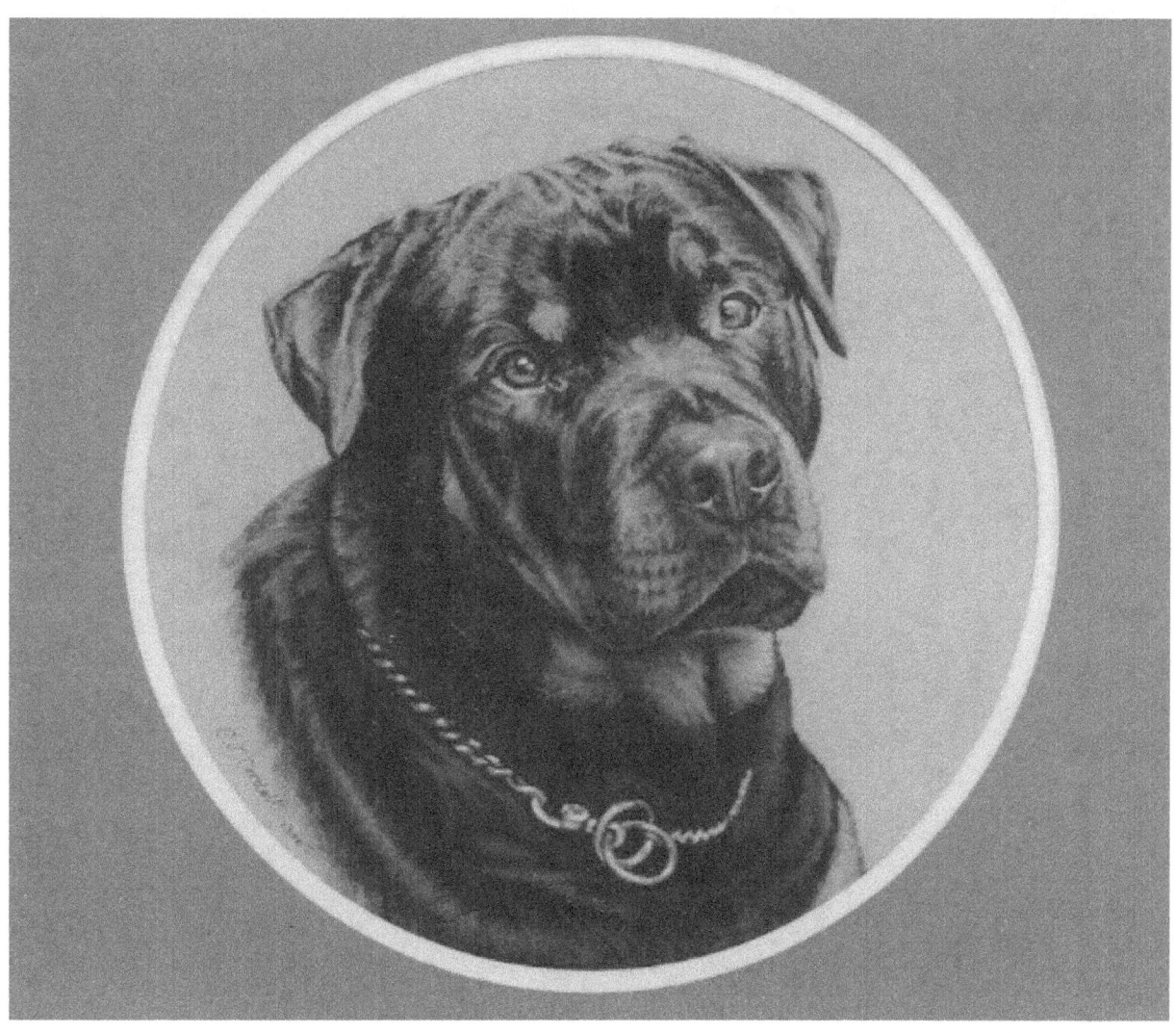

Ziggy the Rottweiler, 1990

m: pastel on paper

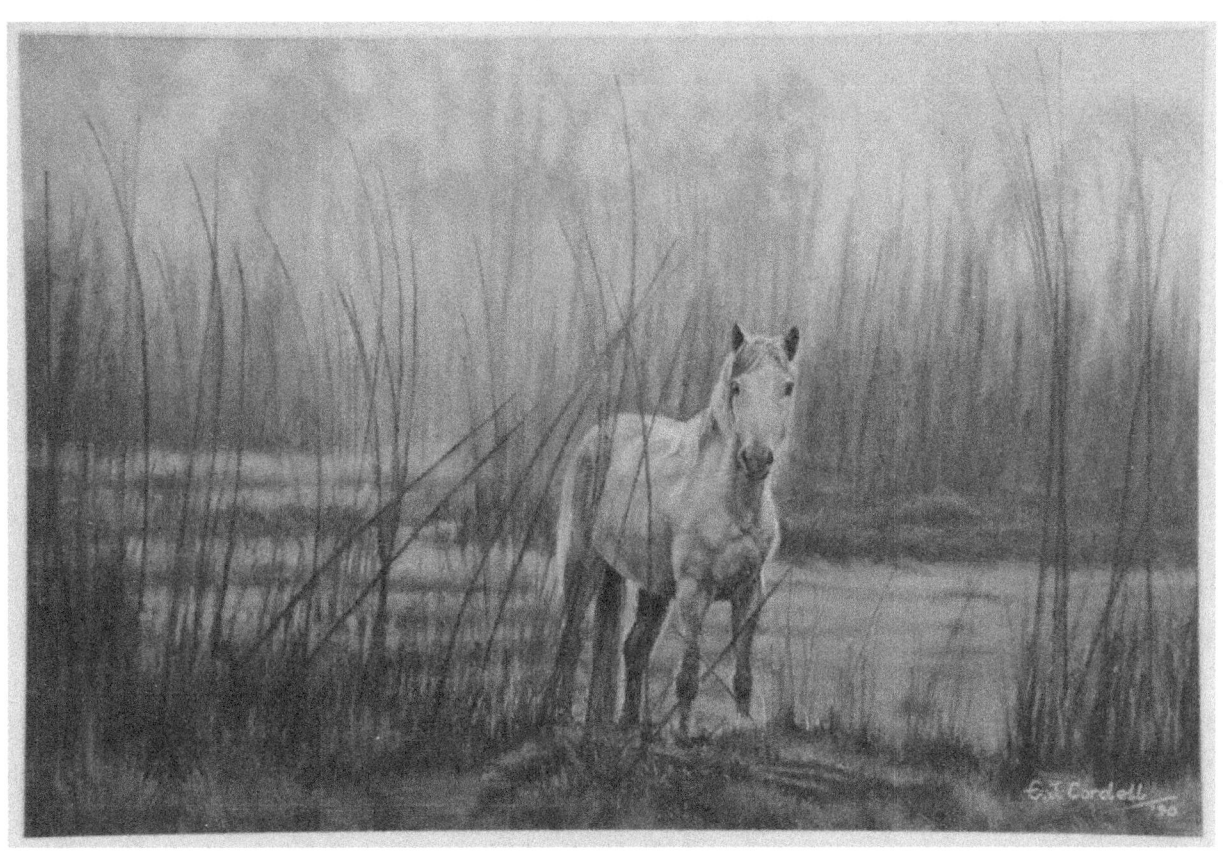

Camargue horse, 1990

m: pastel on paper

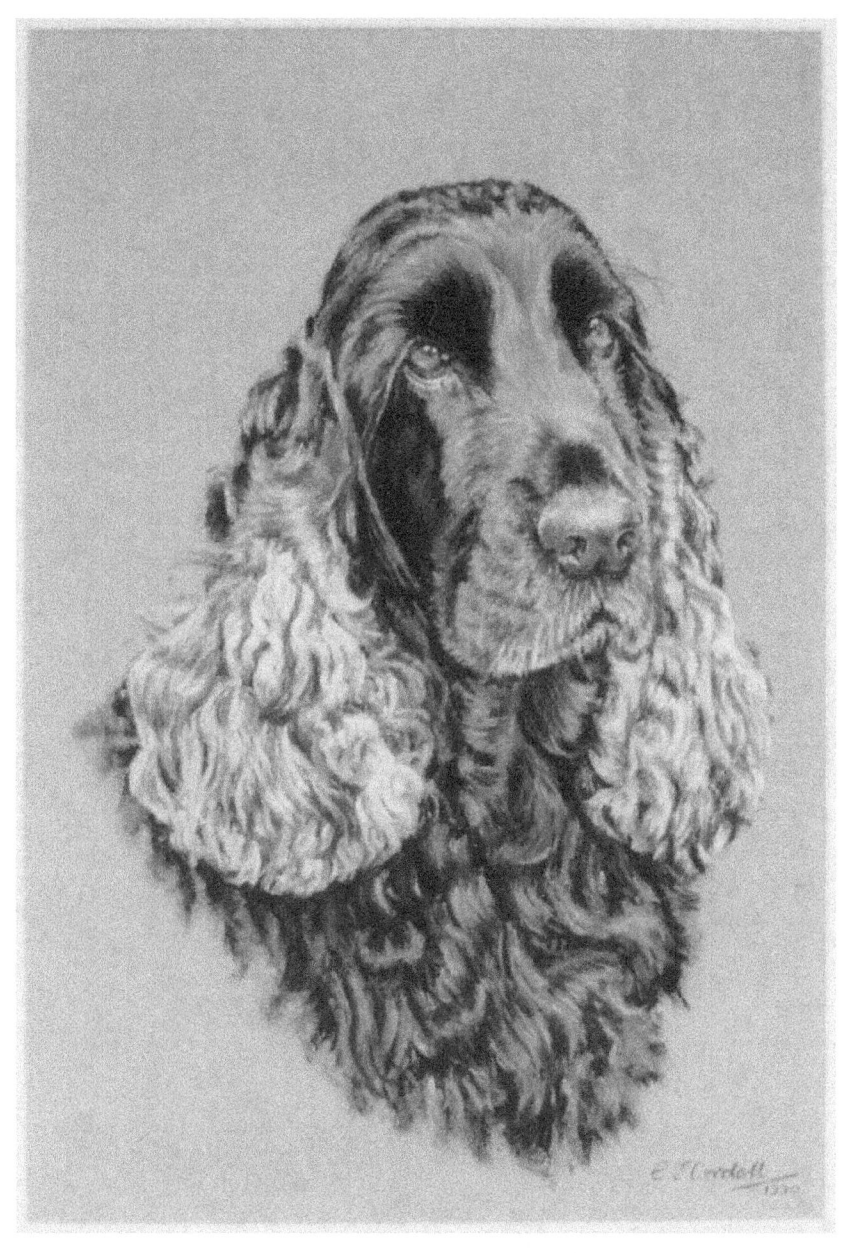

Cockerspaniel, 1990

m: pastel on paper

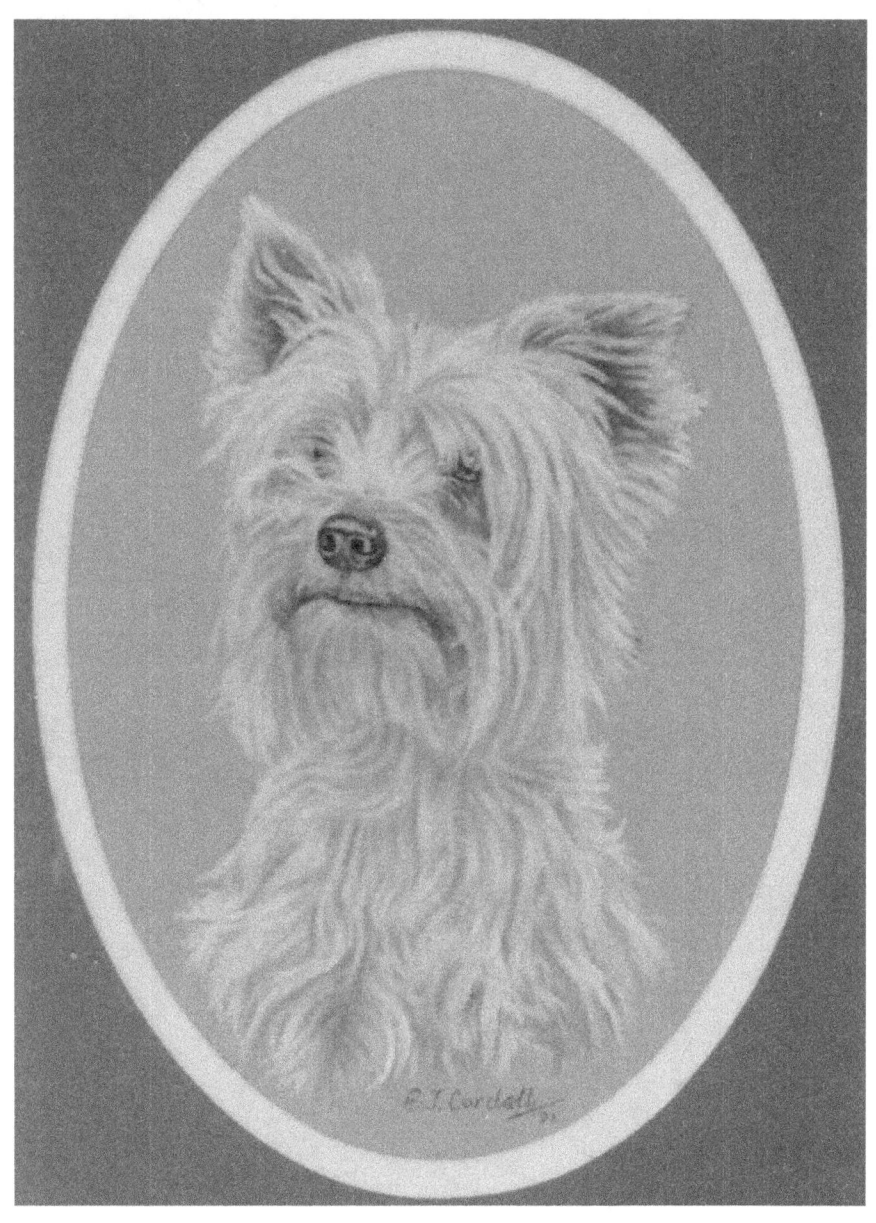

Silky Terrier, 1991
m: pastel on paper

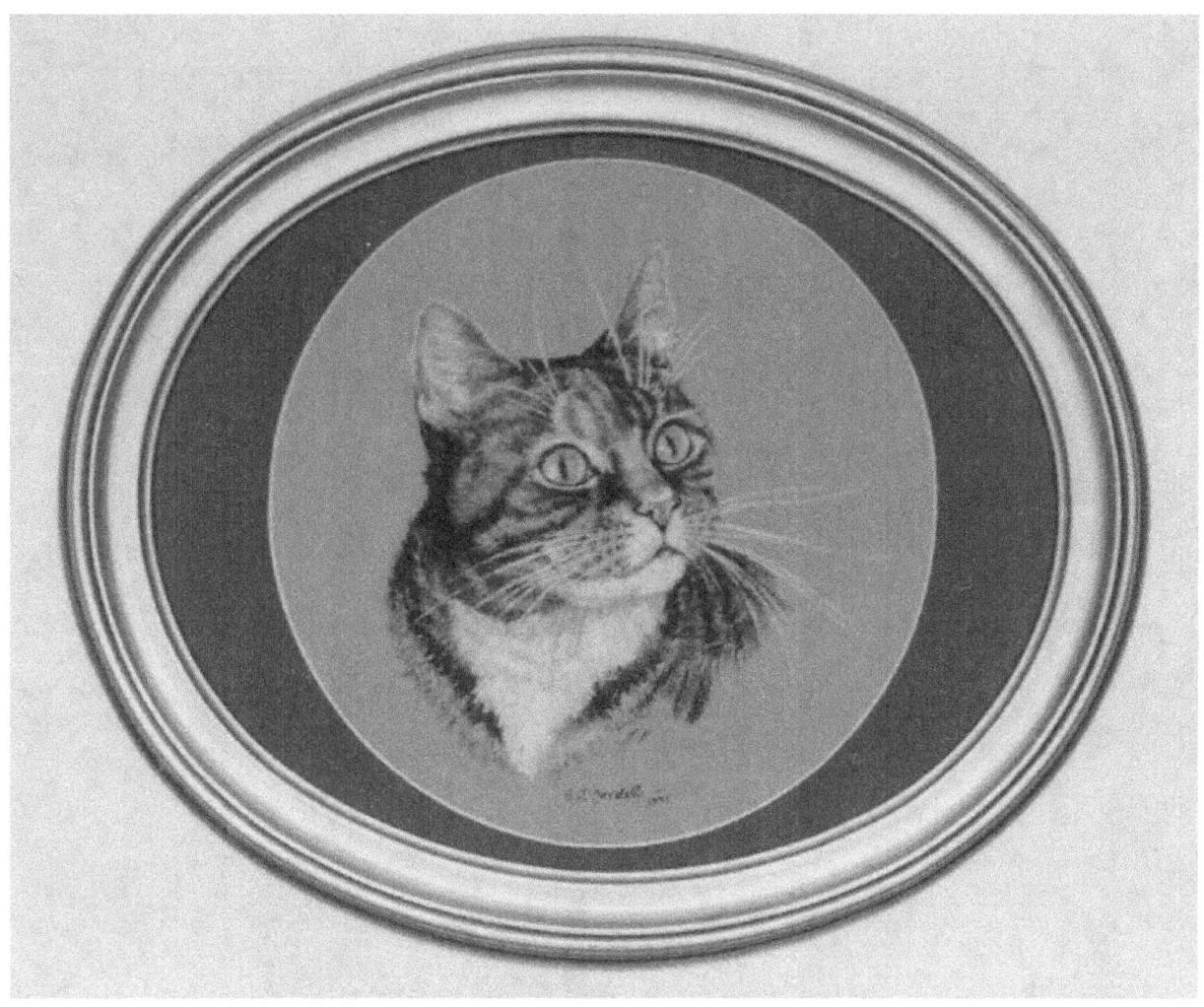

Cat, 1991

m: pastel on paper

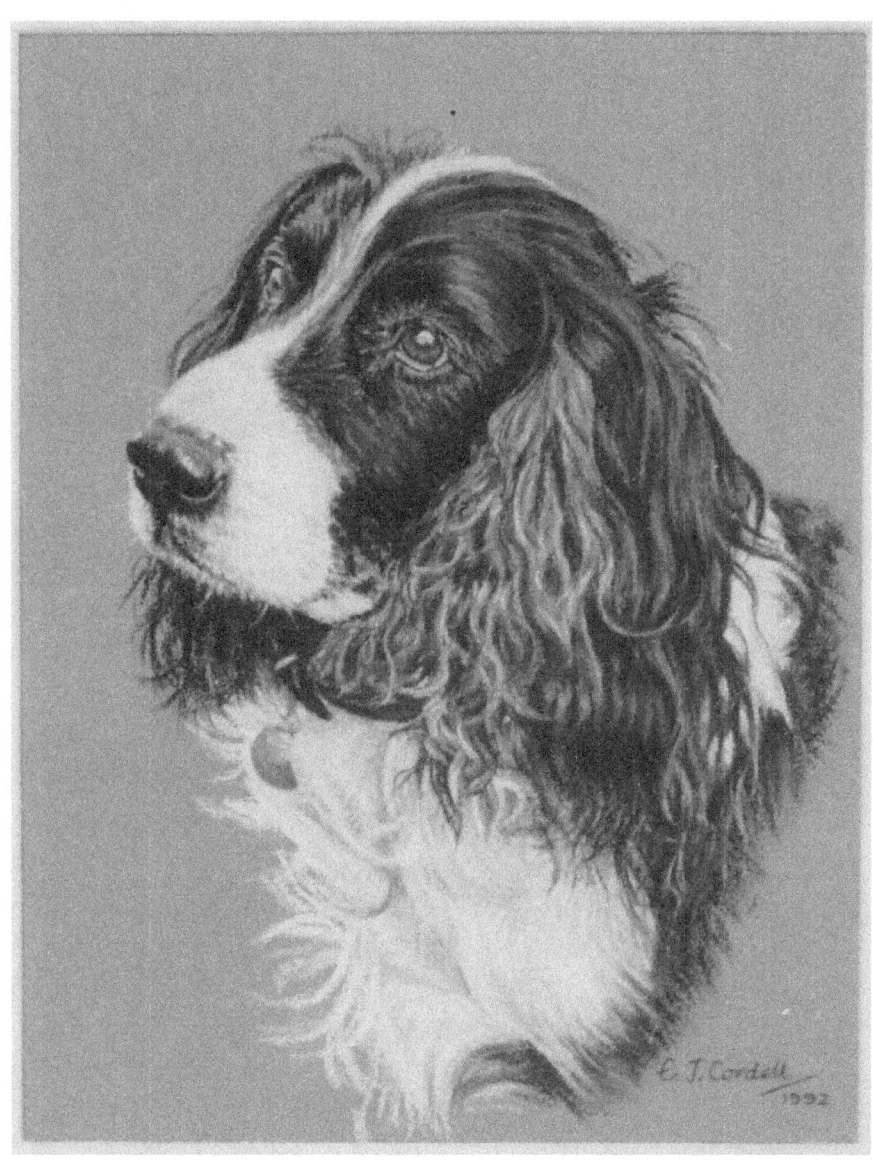

Rowley the Springer Spaniel, 1992
m: pastel on paper

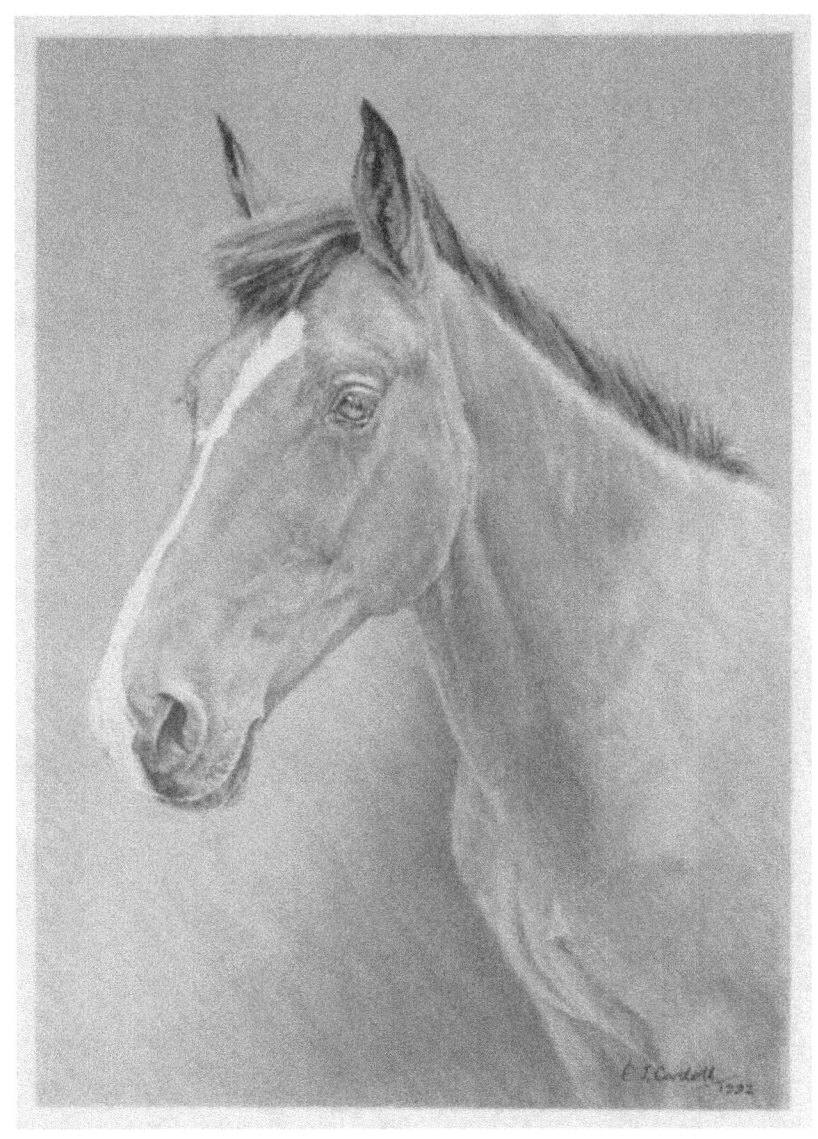

Horse, 1992

m: pastel on paper

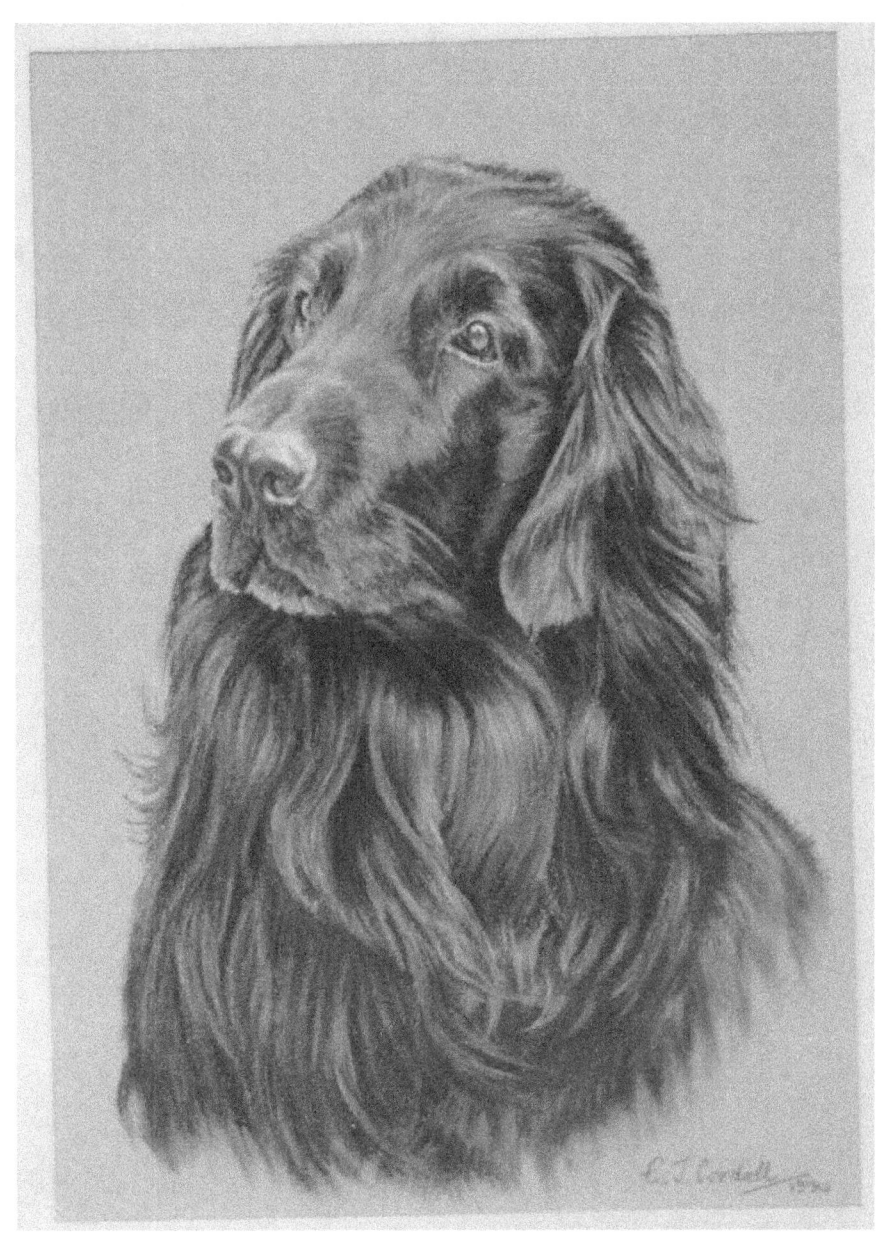

Jet the Black Retriever, 1992

m: pastel on paper

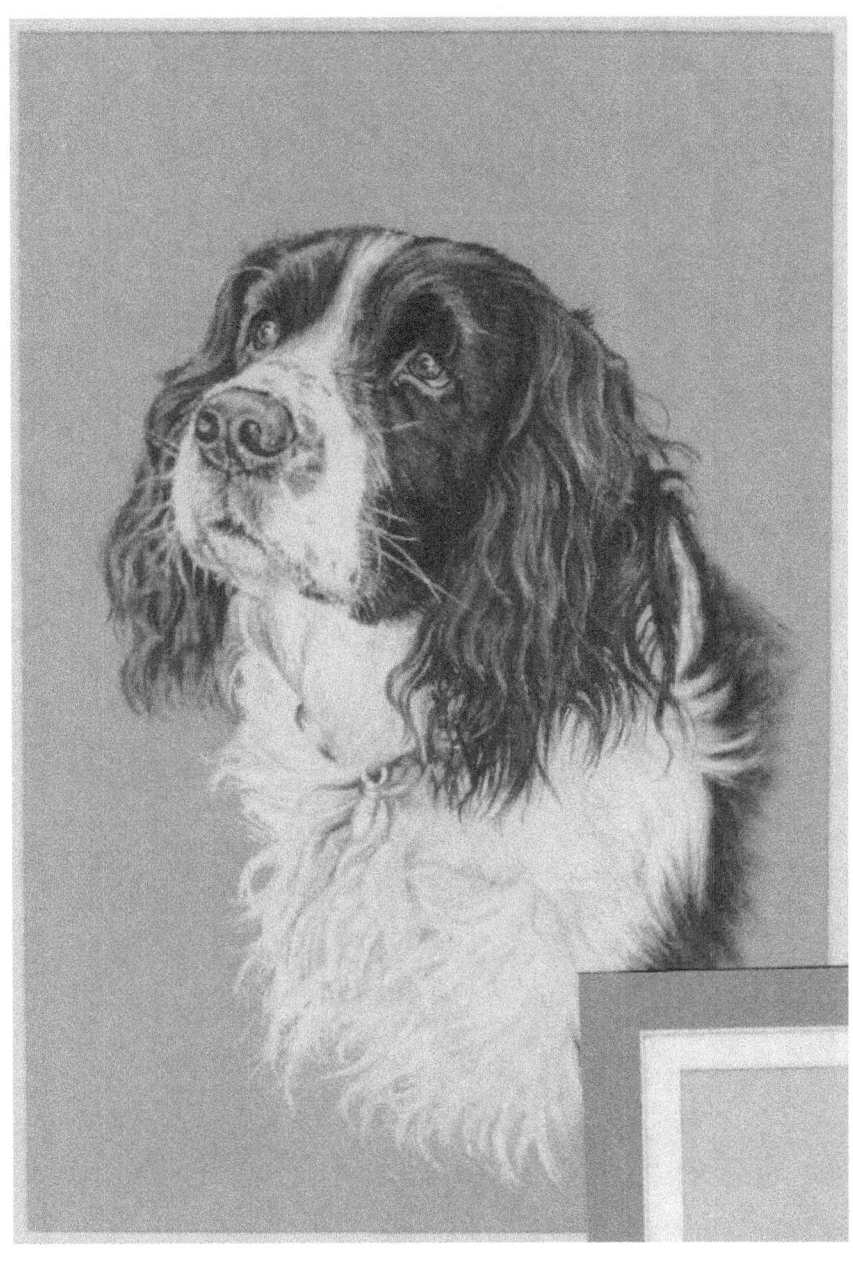

Thomas the Spaniel, 1992
m: Pastel on paper

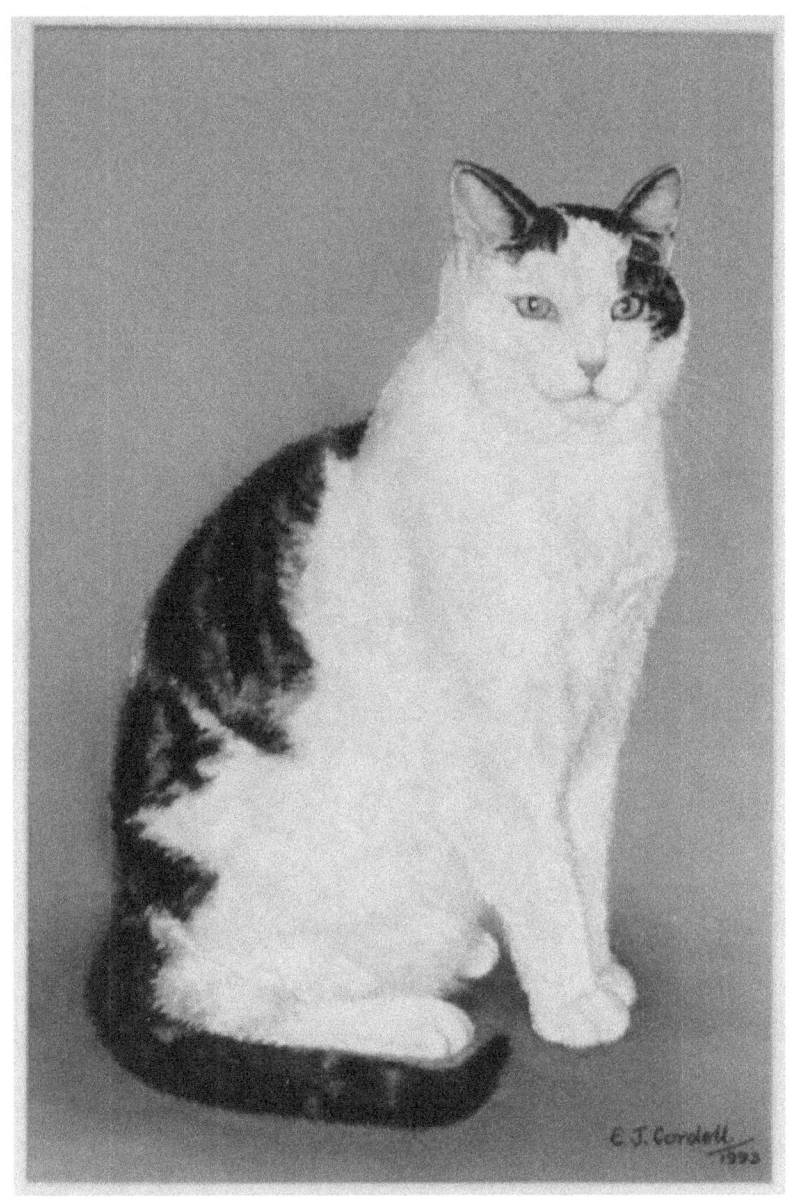

Tortoiseshell Cat, 1993

m: pastel on paper

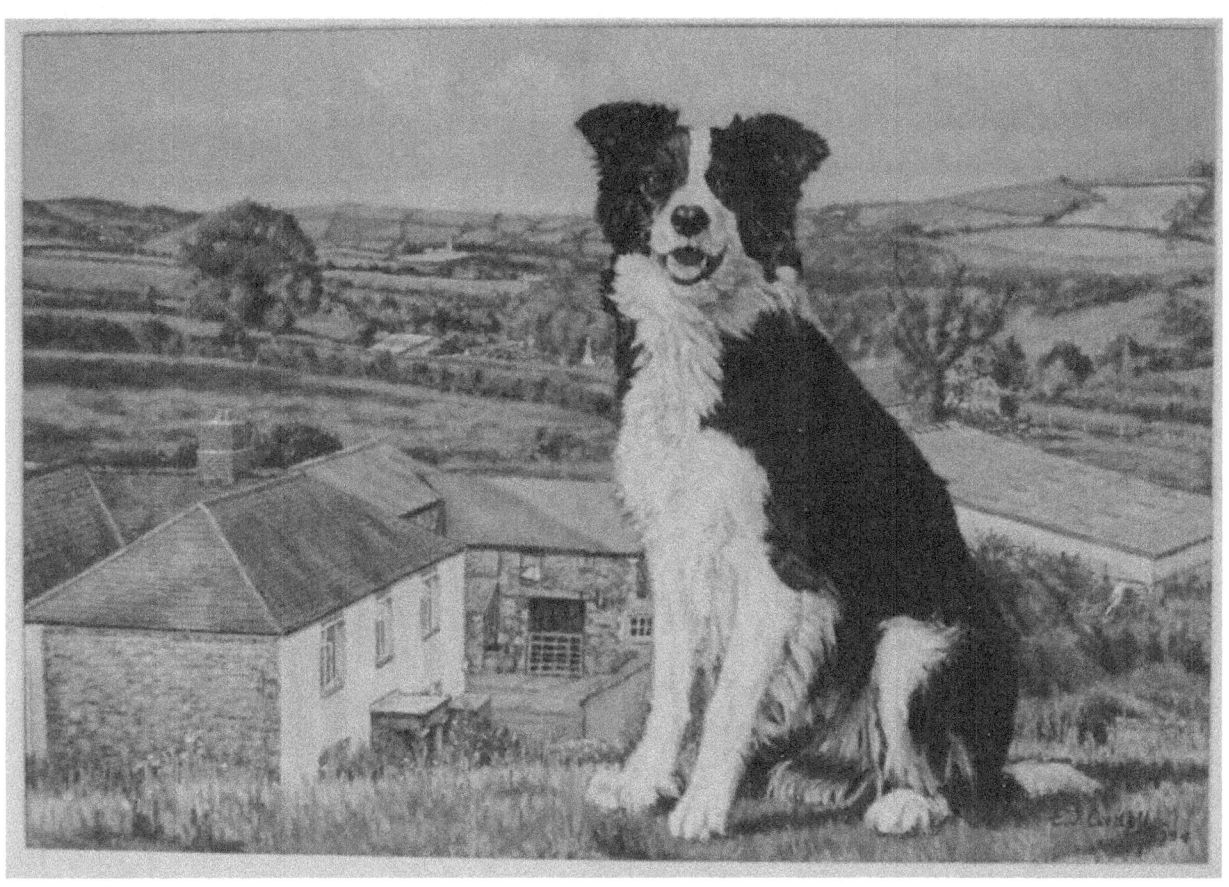

Border Collie at Nurston Farm, 1994

m: pastel on paper

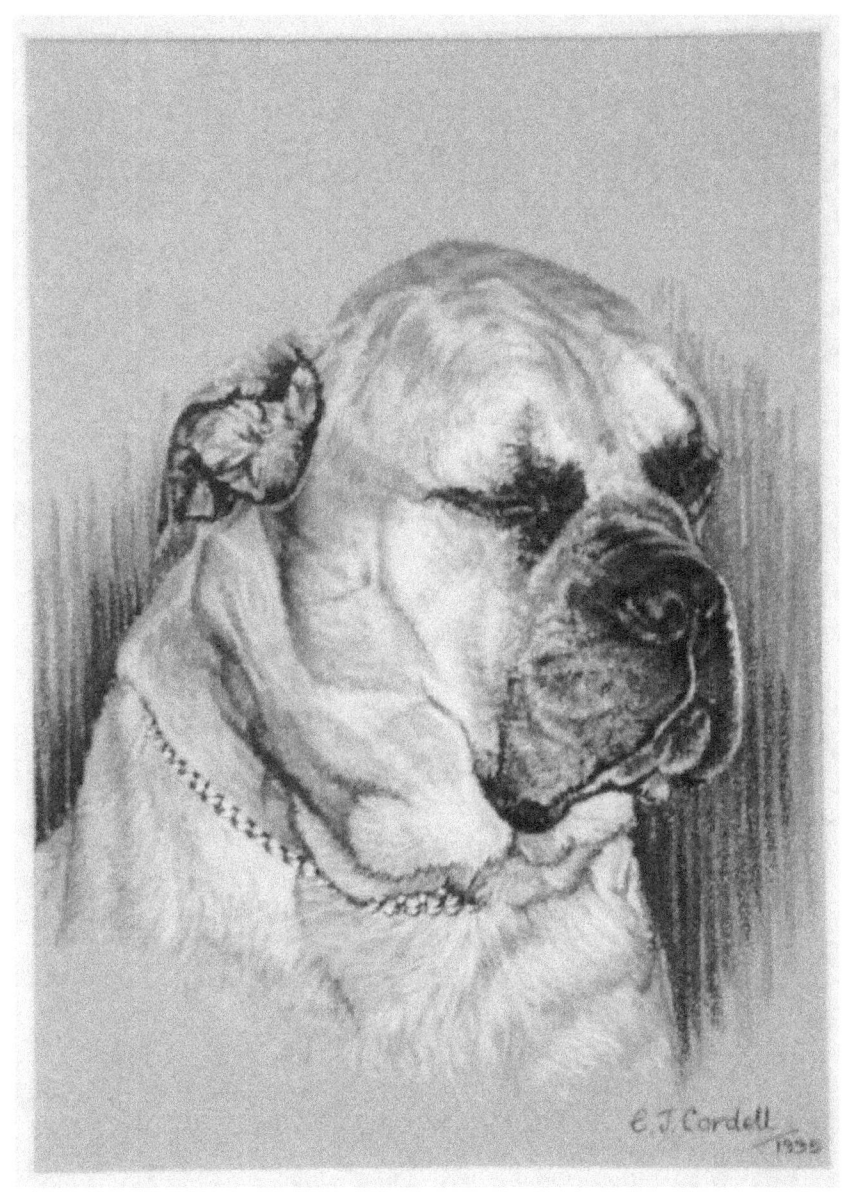

Dog, 1995

m: pastel on paper

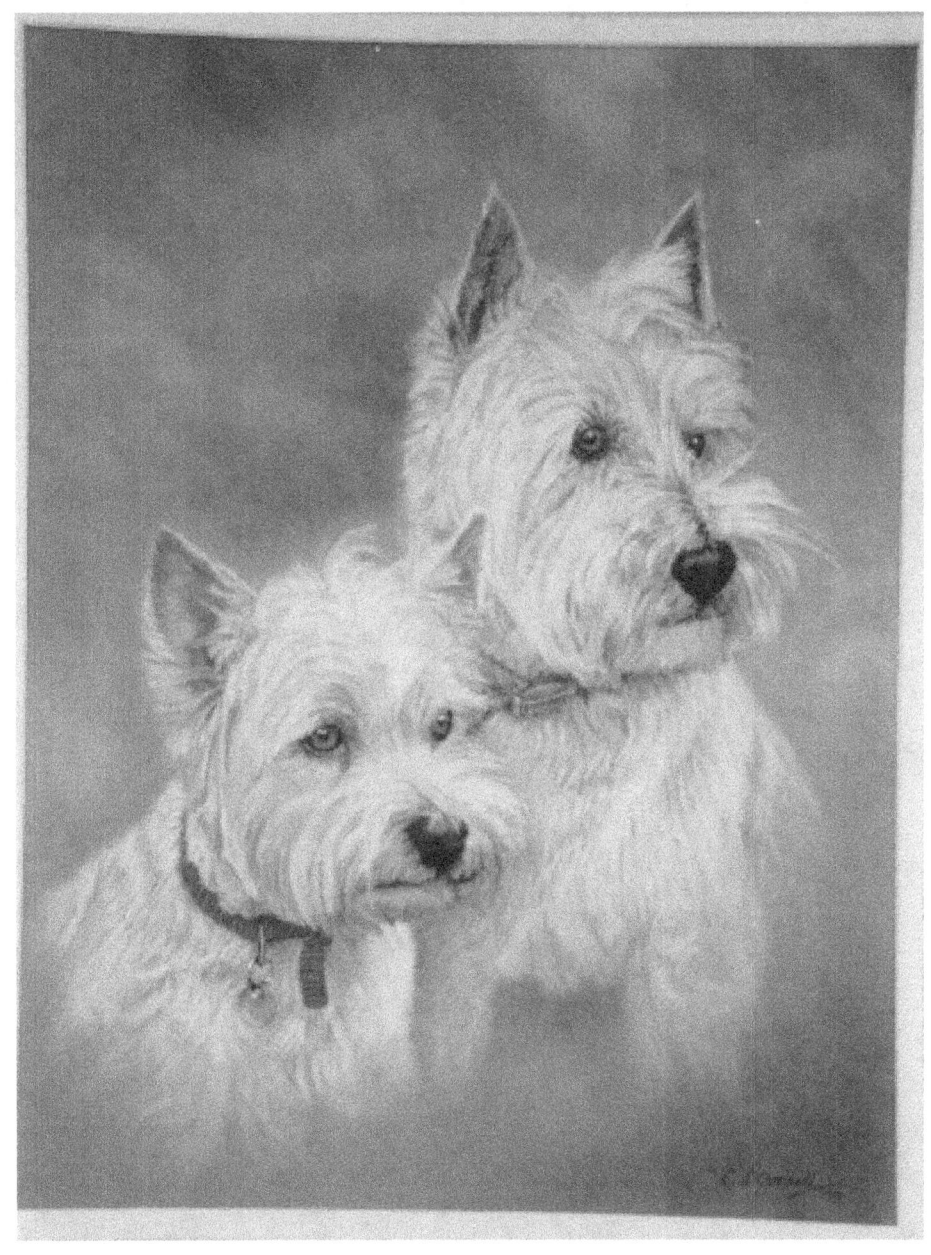

Westies, 1999
m: pastel on paper

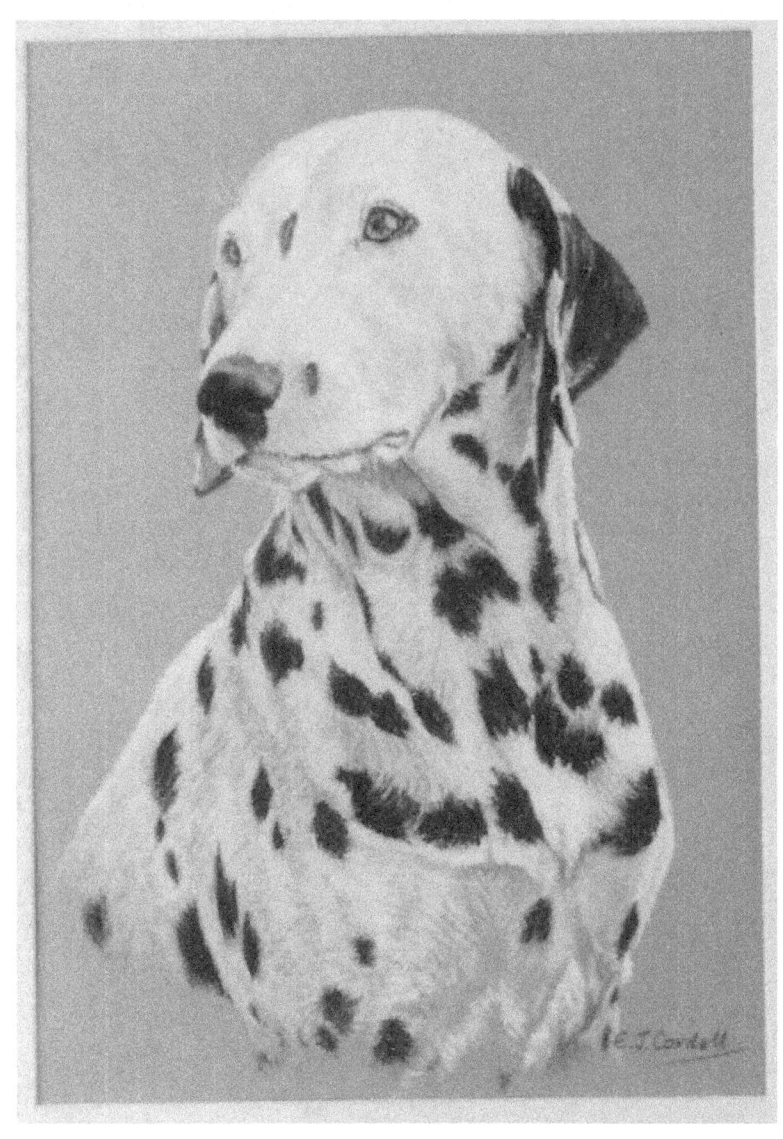

Dalmatian, 2001

m: pastel on paper

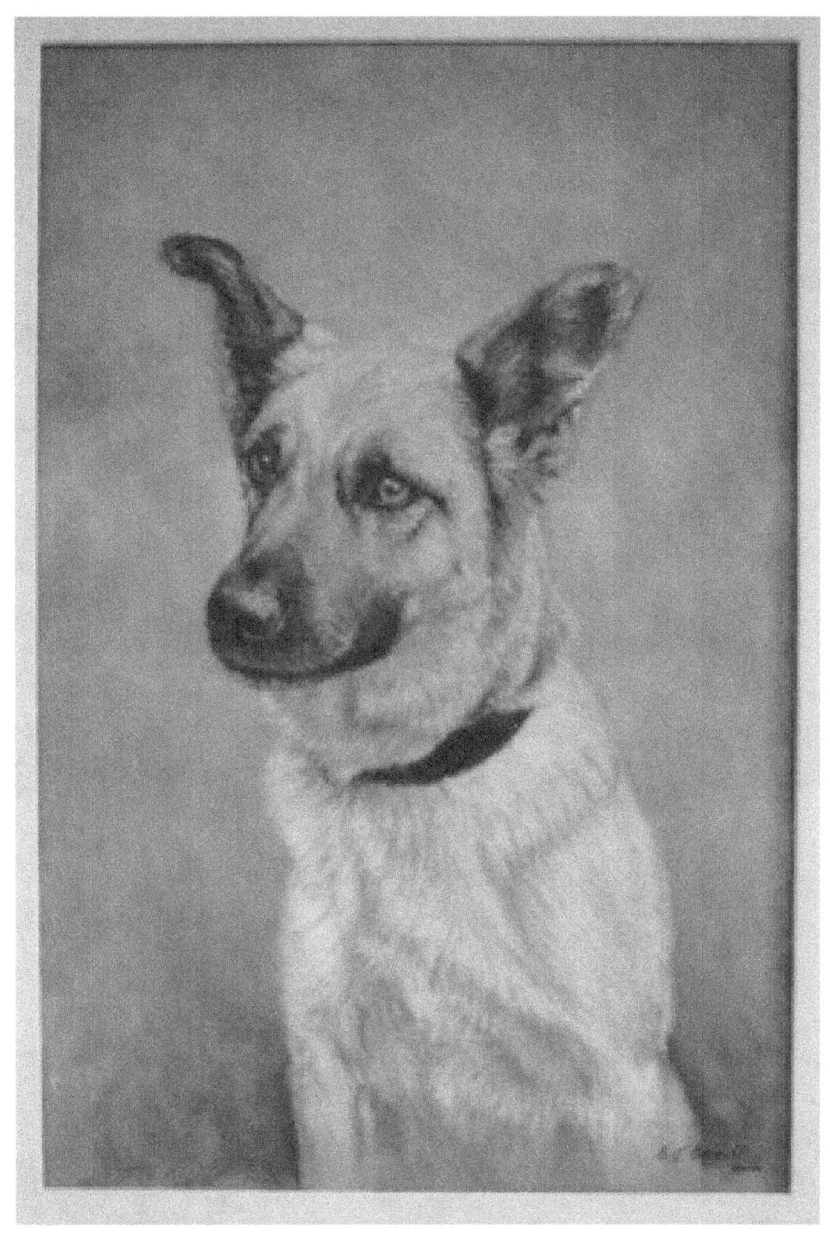

Dog, 2001
m: pastel on paper

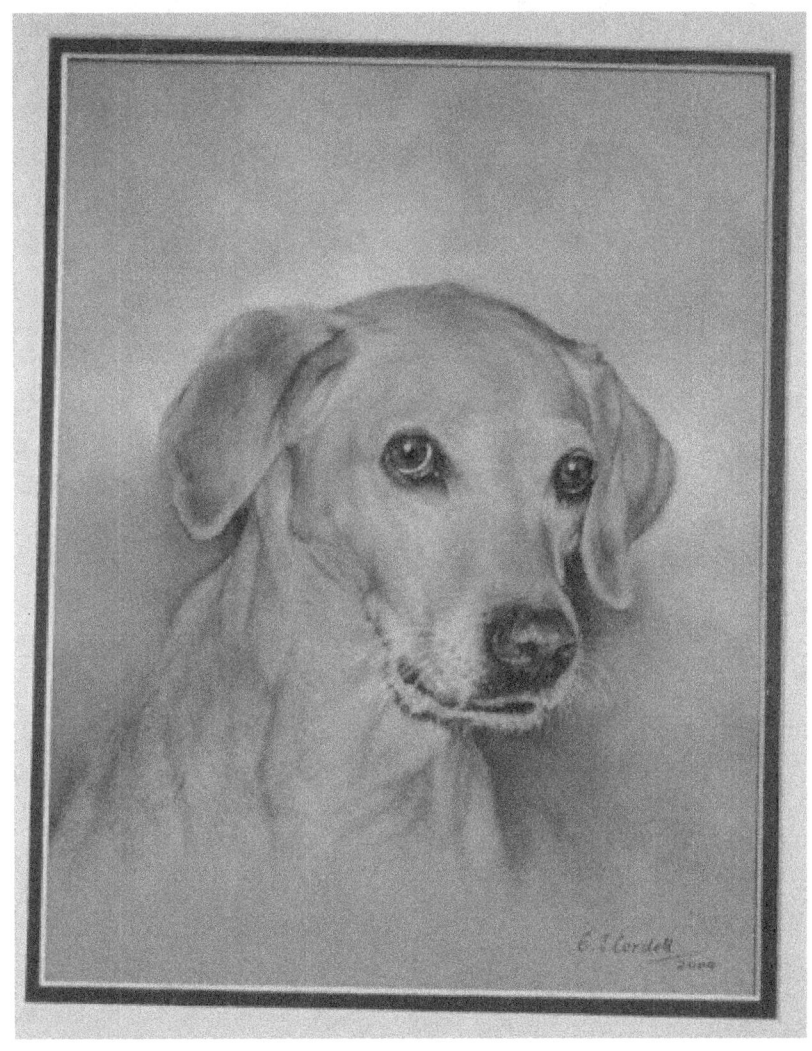

Dog, 2004
m: pastel on paper

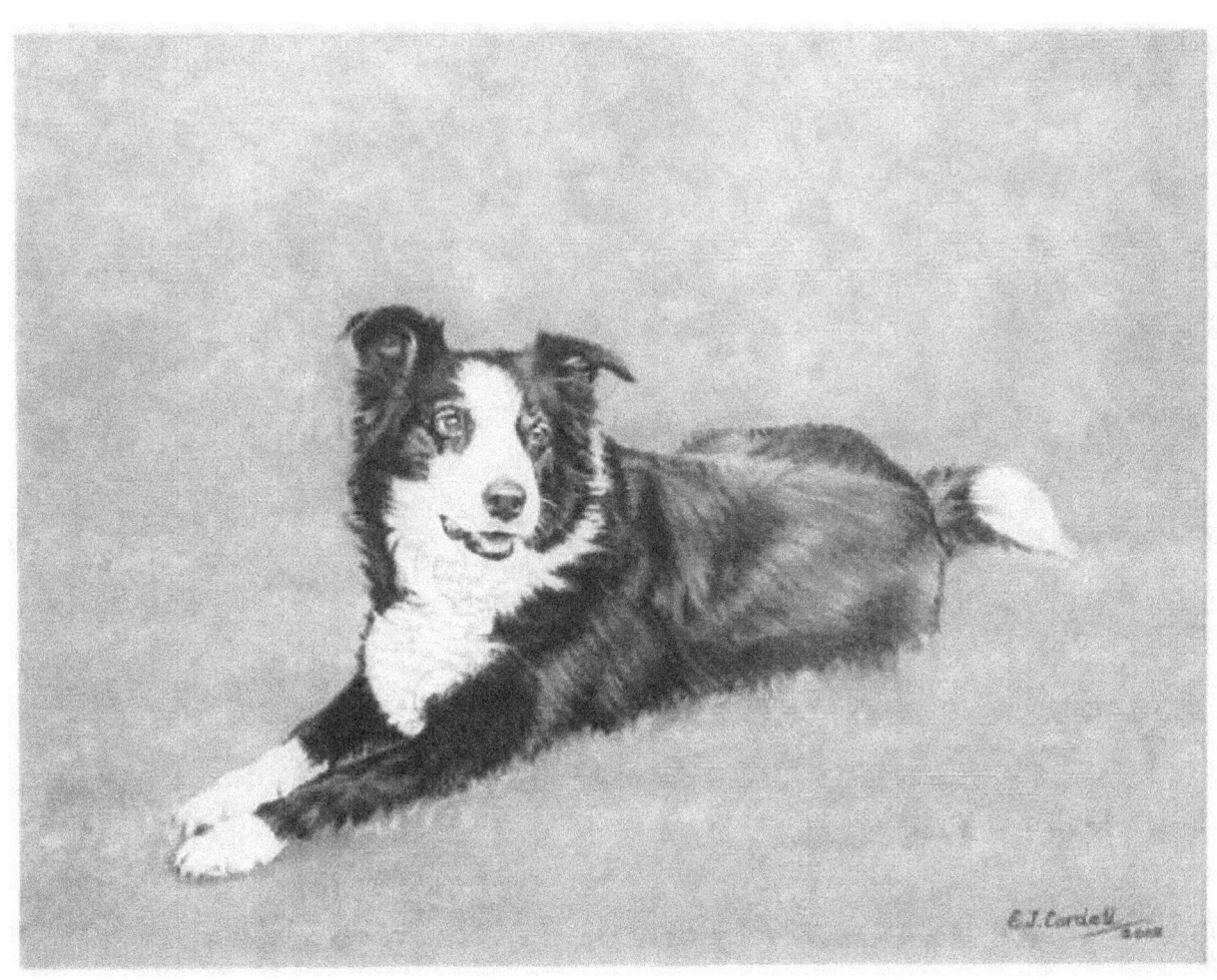

Border Collie, 2008
m: pastel on paper

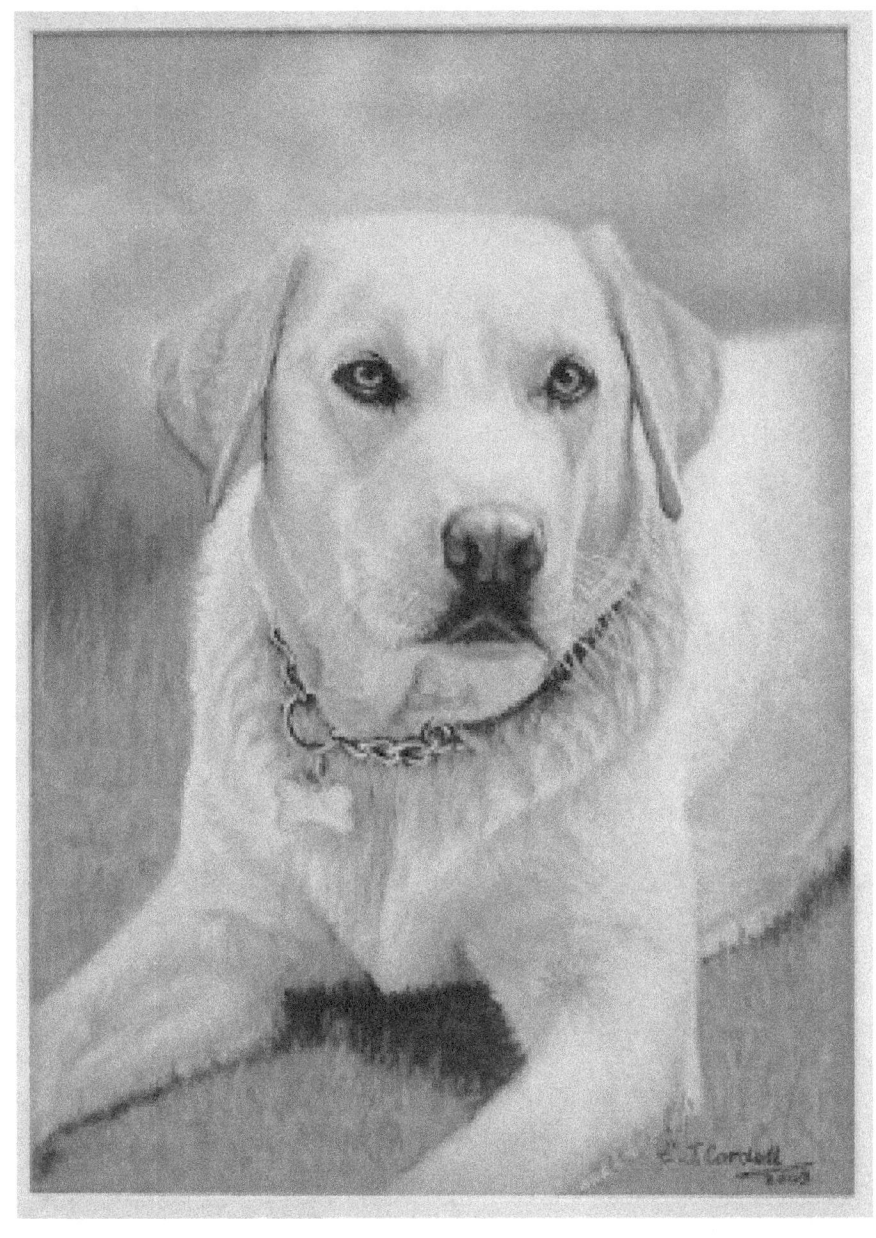

Labrador, 2009
m: pastel on paper

4 ABSTRACTS

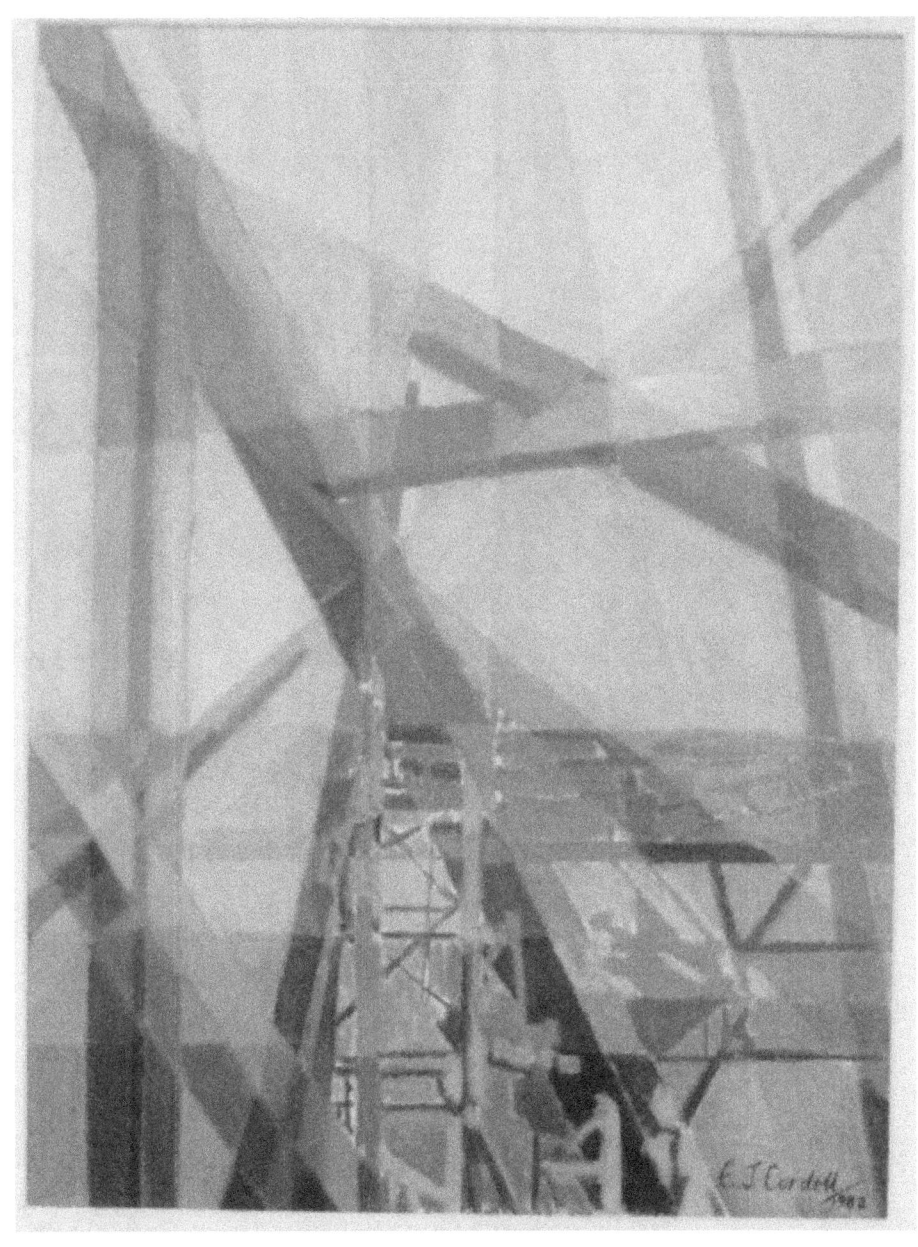

Girders, 1982

m: pastel on paper

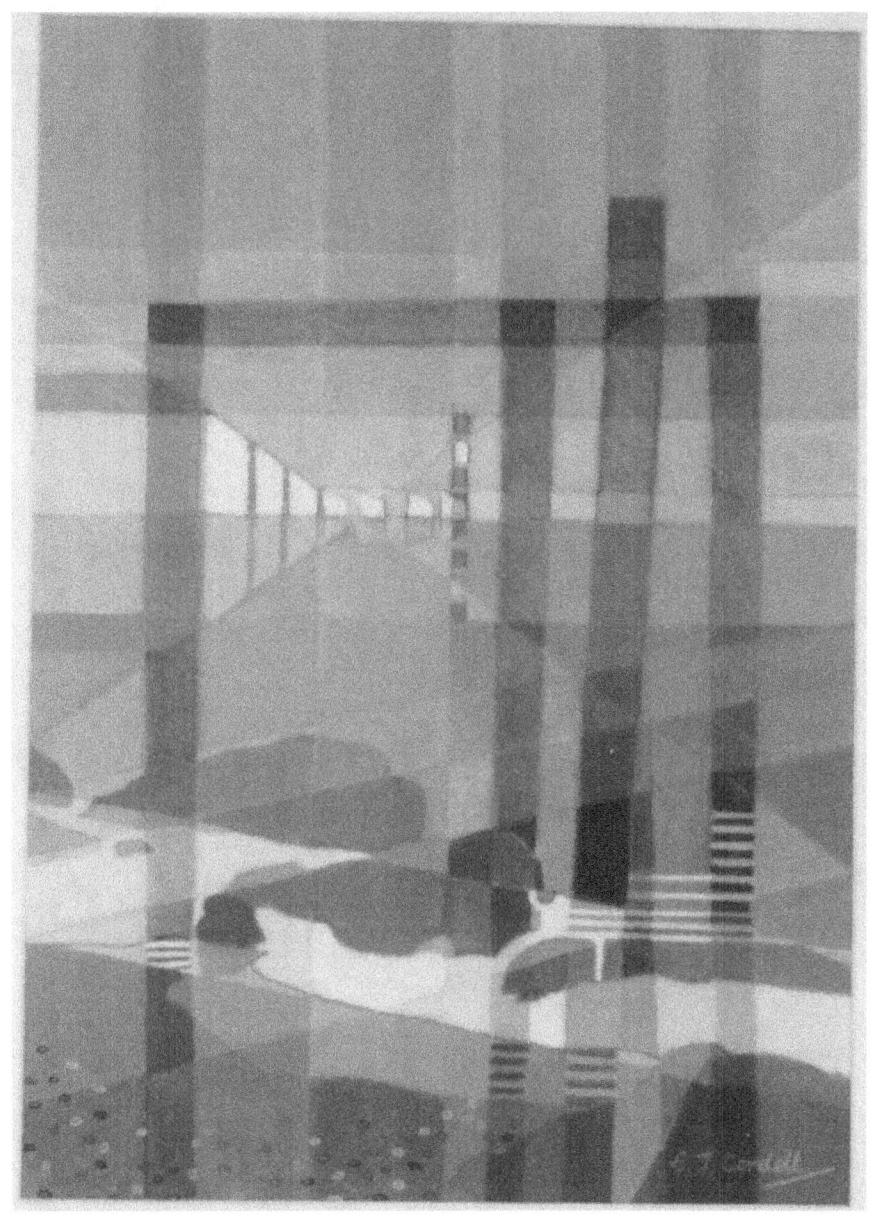

Needles Lighthouse, Isle of Wight, 1996

m: pastel on paper

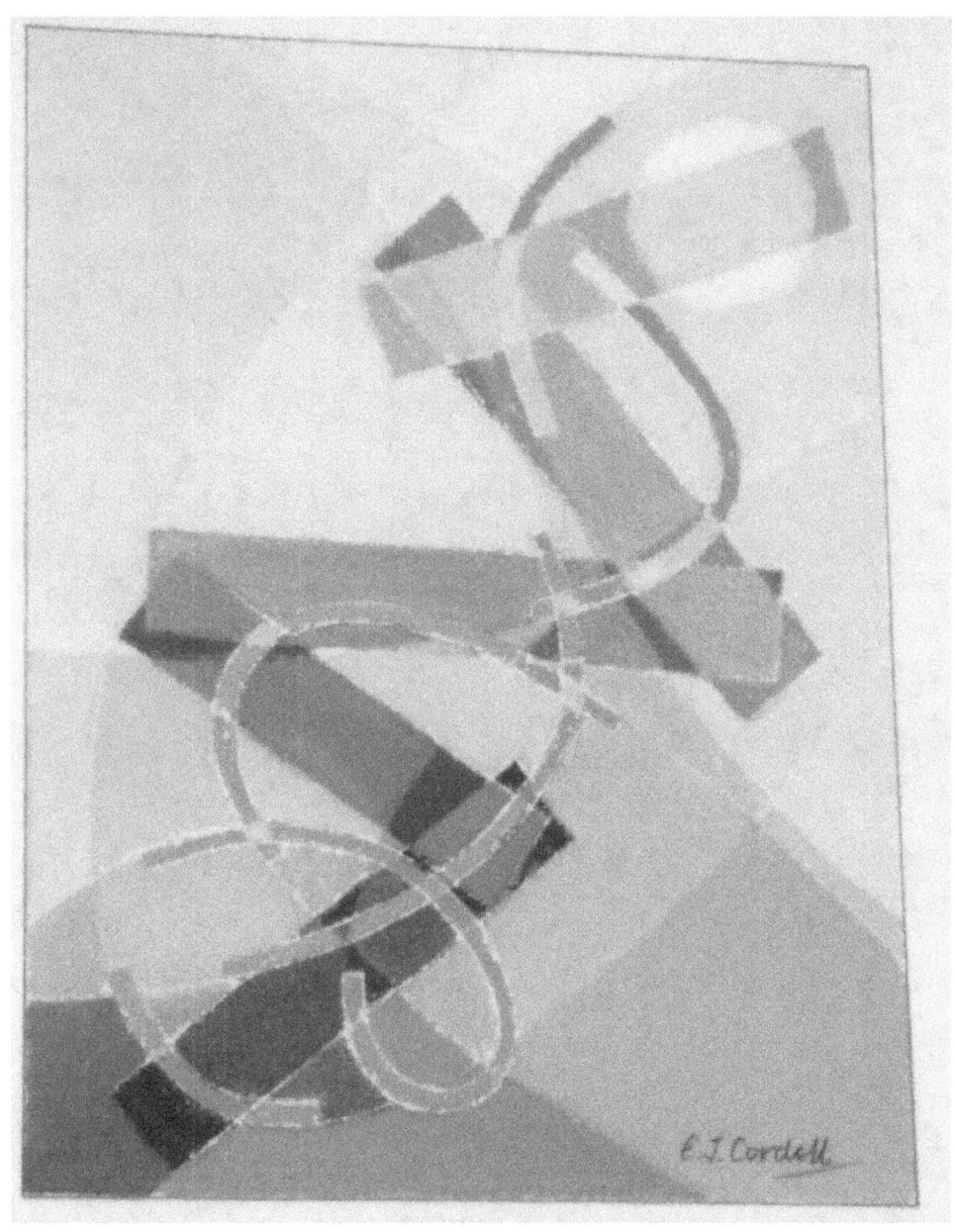

Abstract, date unknown

m: pastel on paper

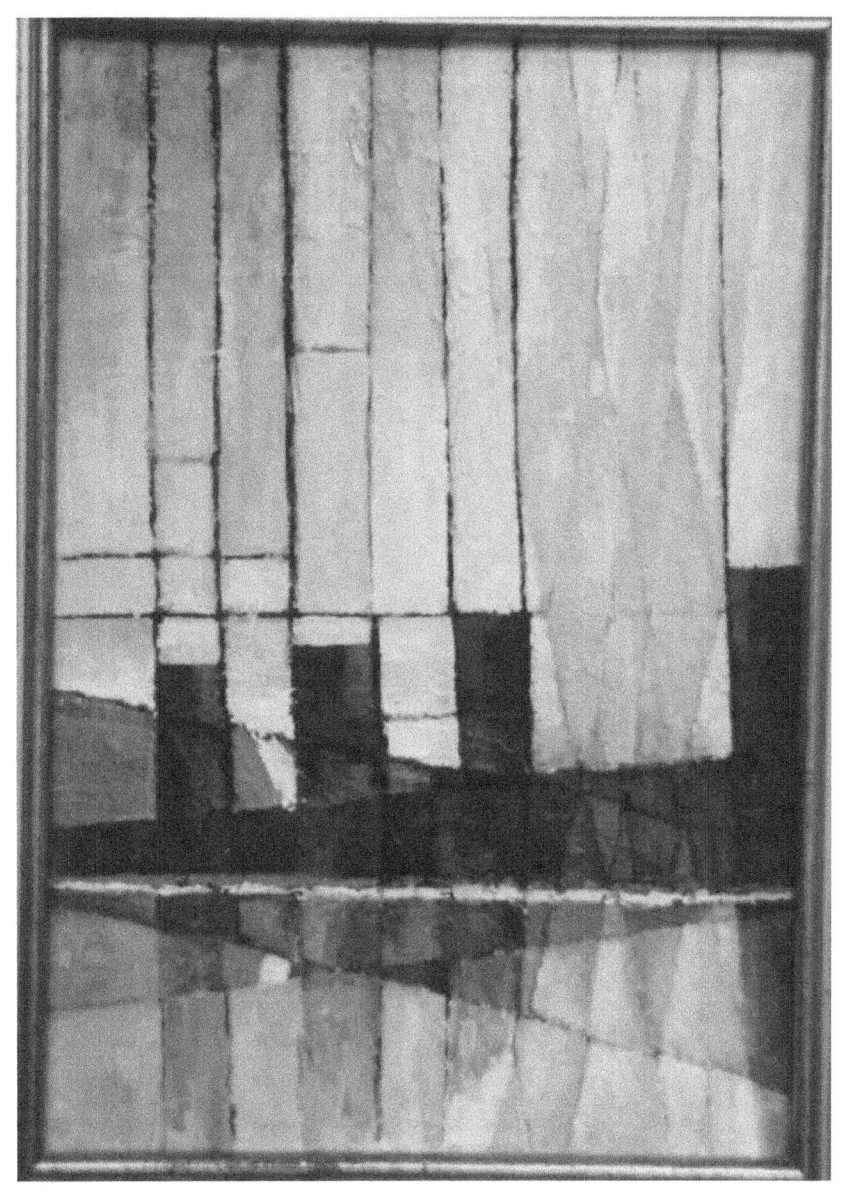

Reflections, date unknown

m: Oil on canvas

5 CHARCOALS

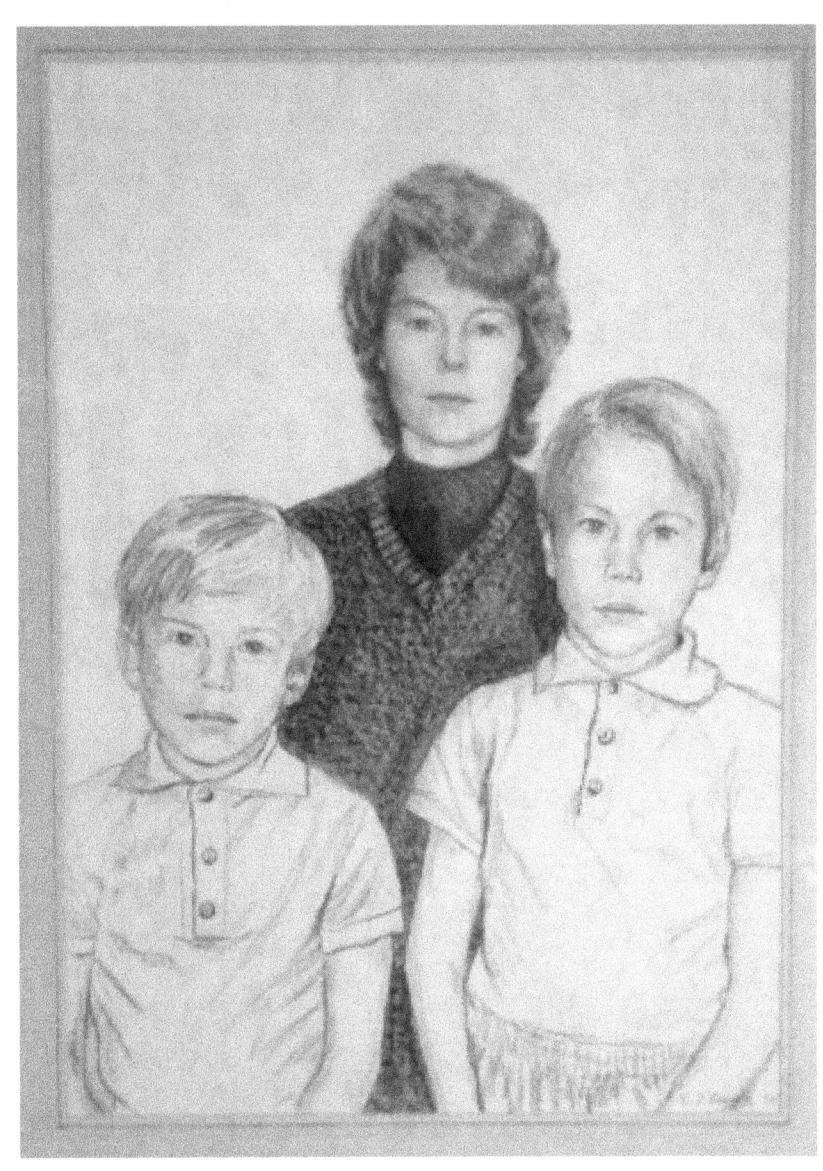

Eileen, Steven and Richard, 1977

m: charcoal on paper

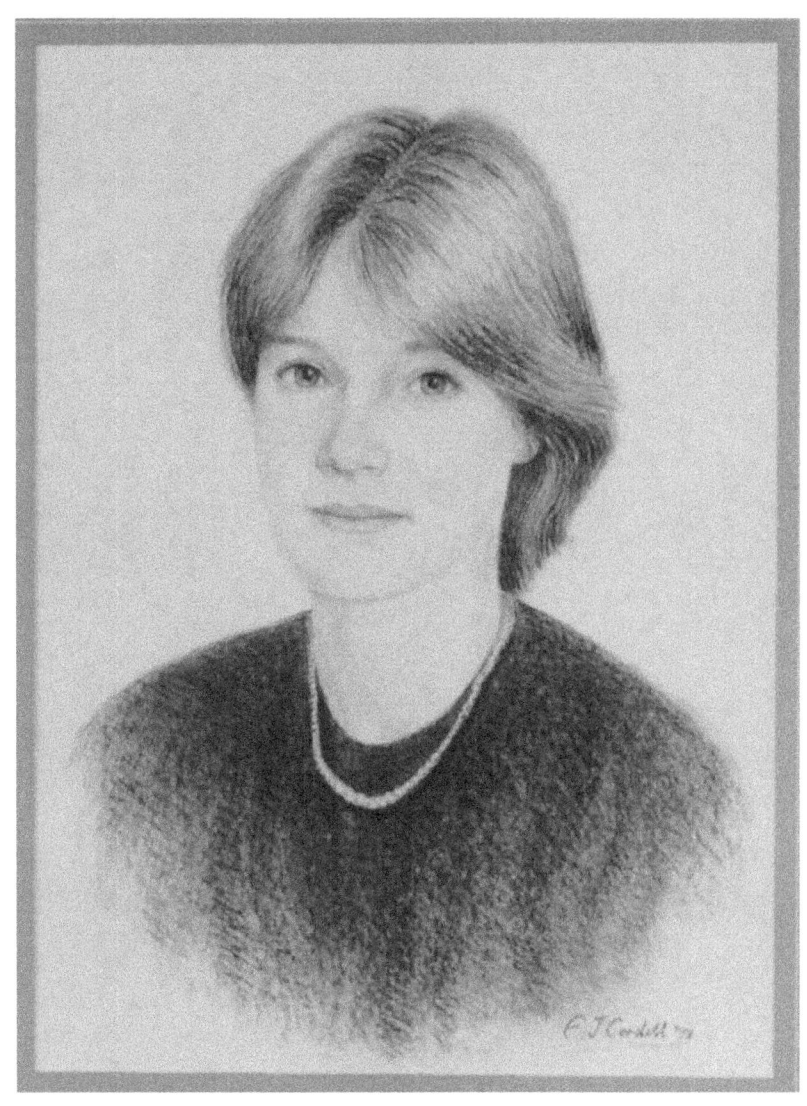

Sasha, 1979

m: charcoal on paper

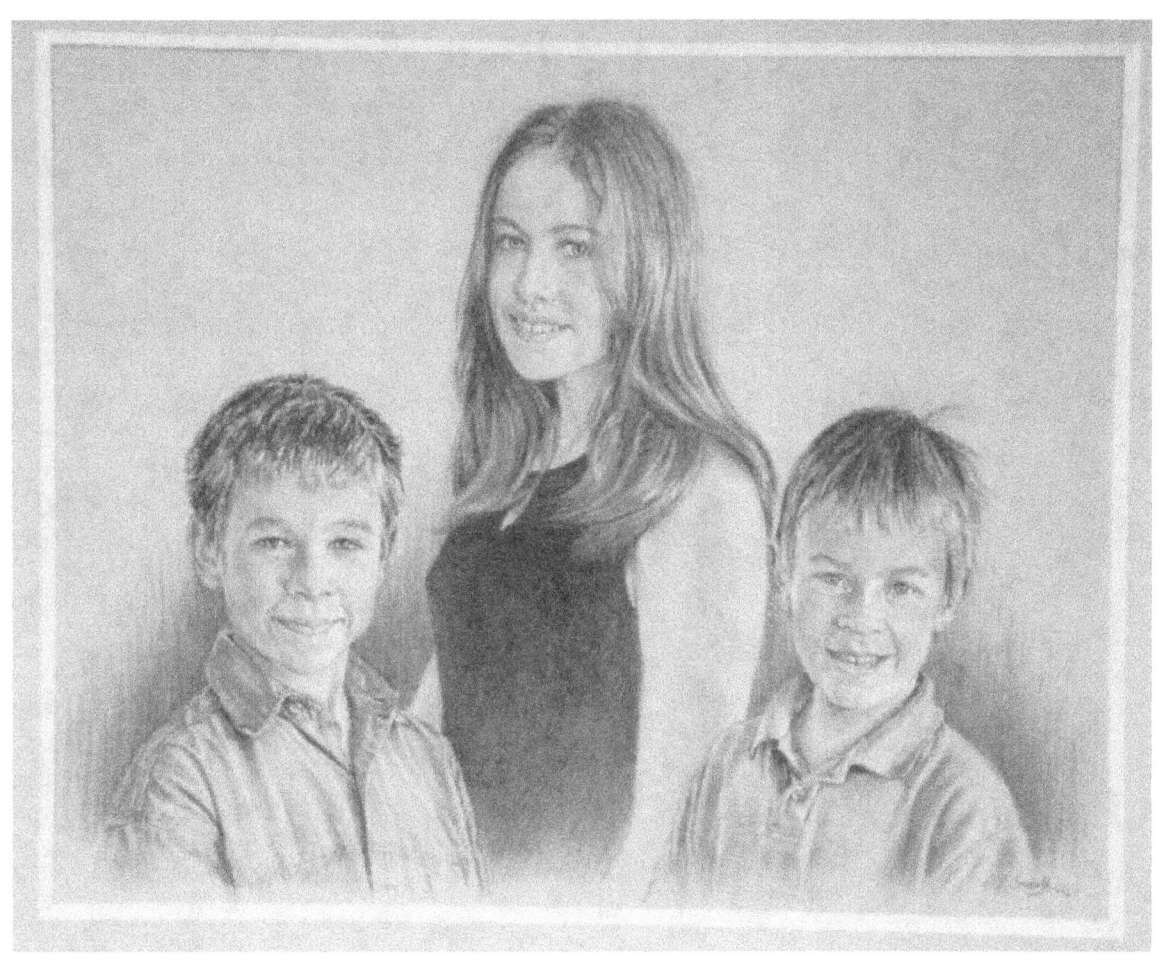

Jessica, James and Tristan, 1996
m: black and white conte on paper

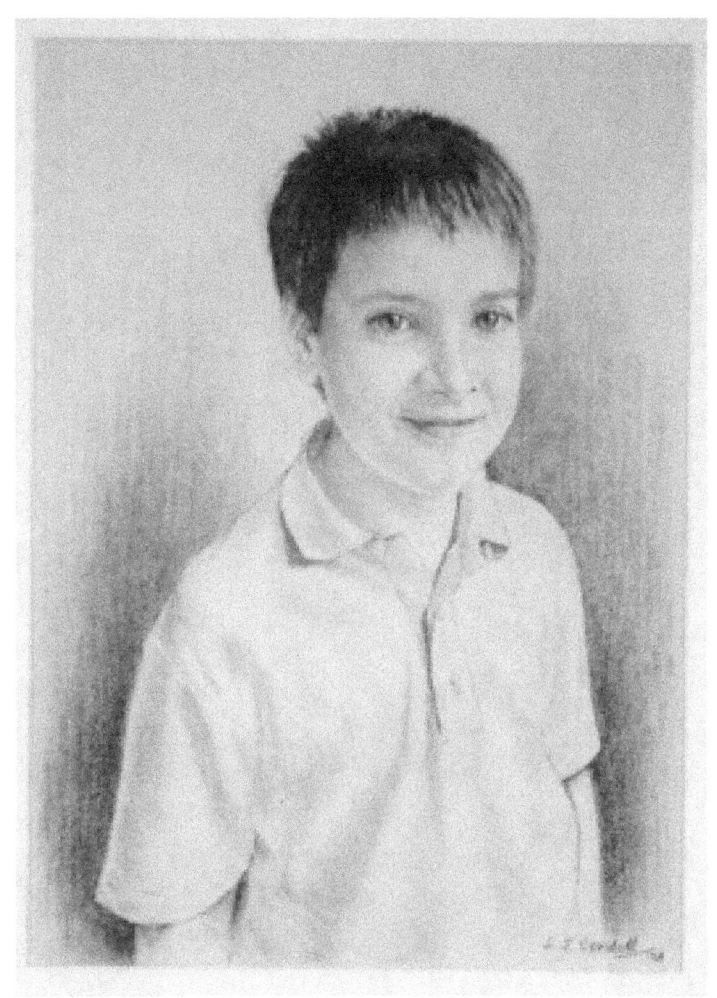

Boy, 2008

m: charcoal on paper

6 ILLUSTRATIONS

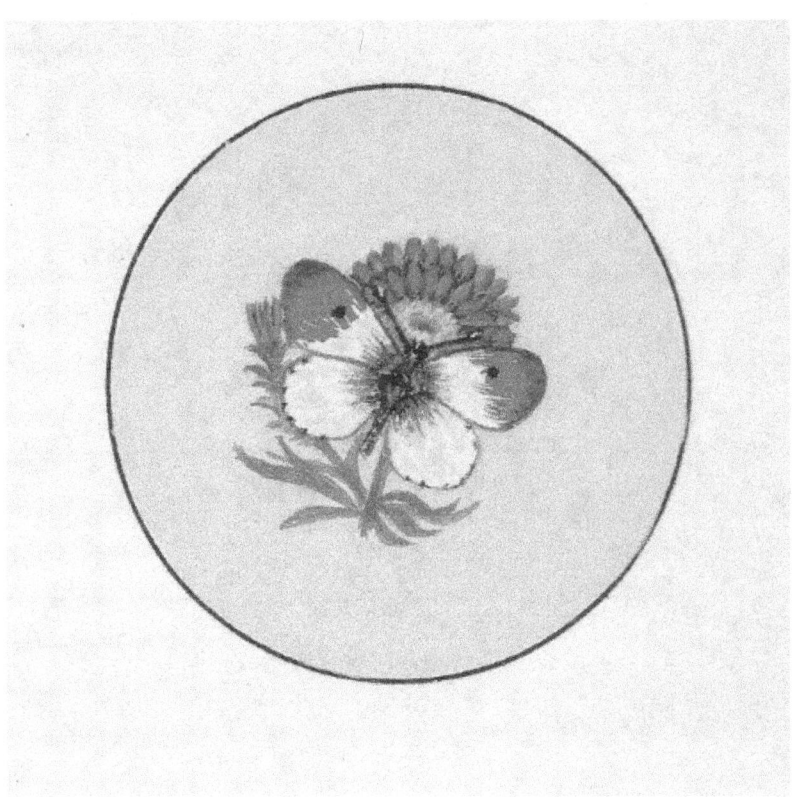

Butterfly illustration for pin-on badge, date unknown

m: pastel on paper

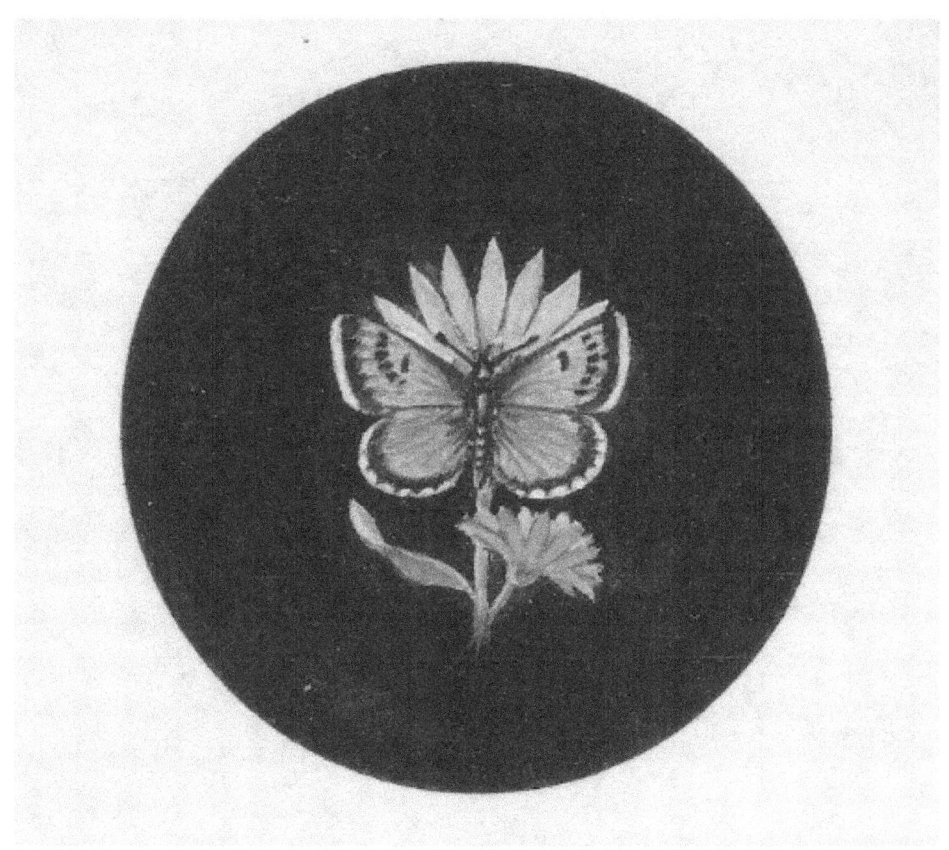

Butterfly illustration for pin-on badge, date unknown

m: pastel on paper

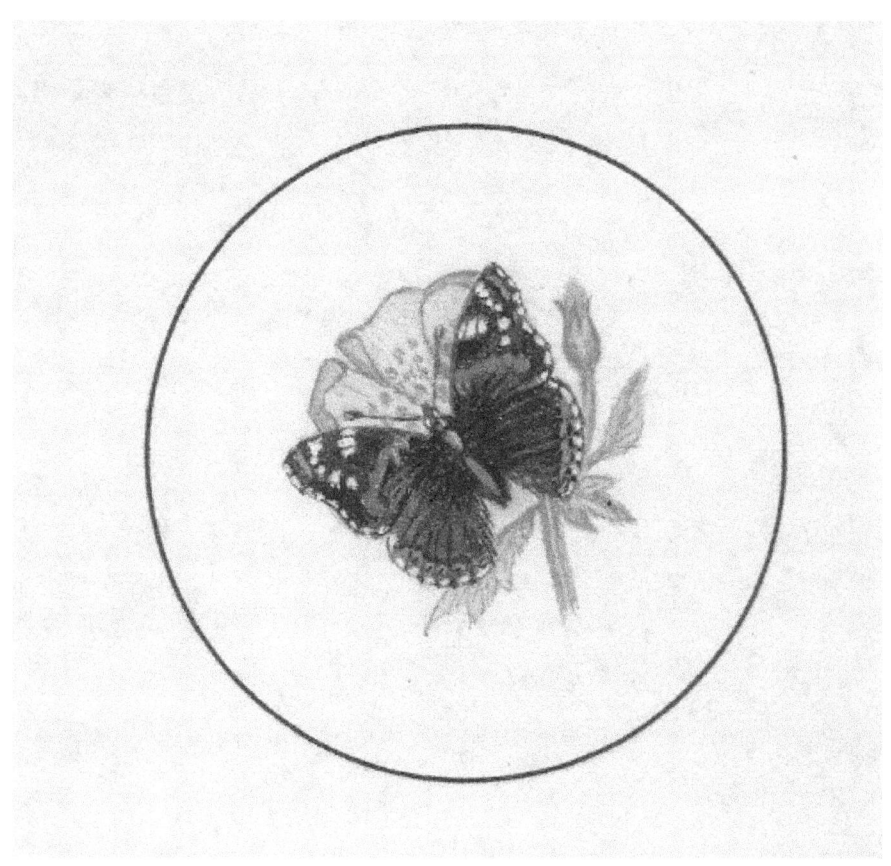

Butterfly illustration for pin-on badge, date unknown

m: pastel on paper

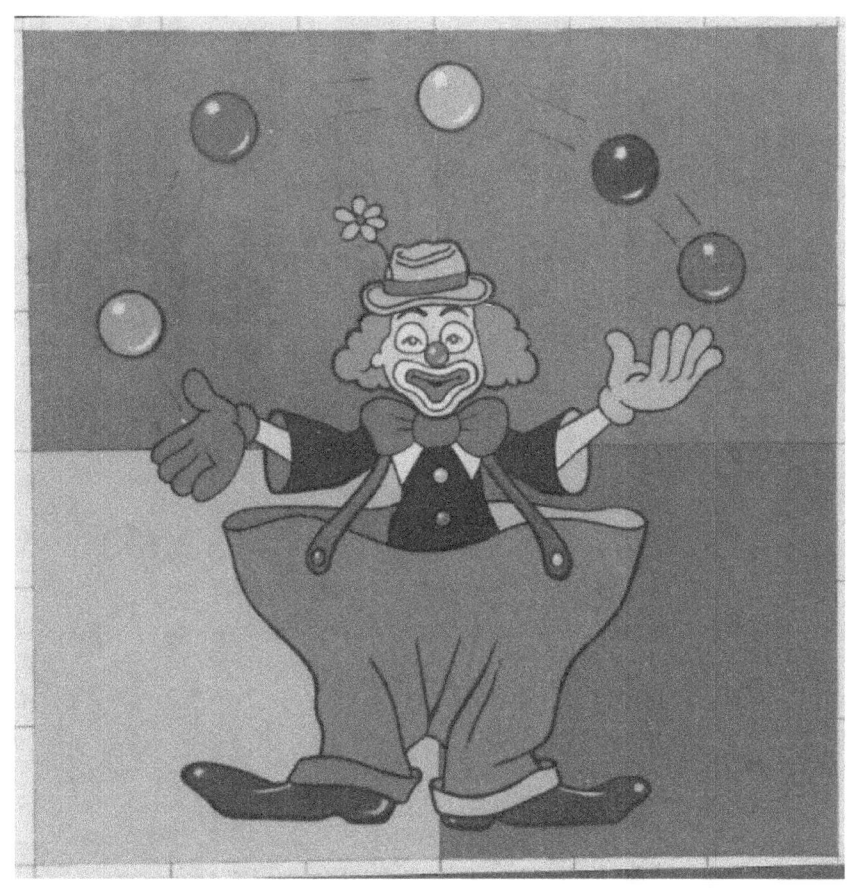

Clown, date unknown

m: felt pen on paper

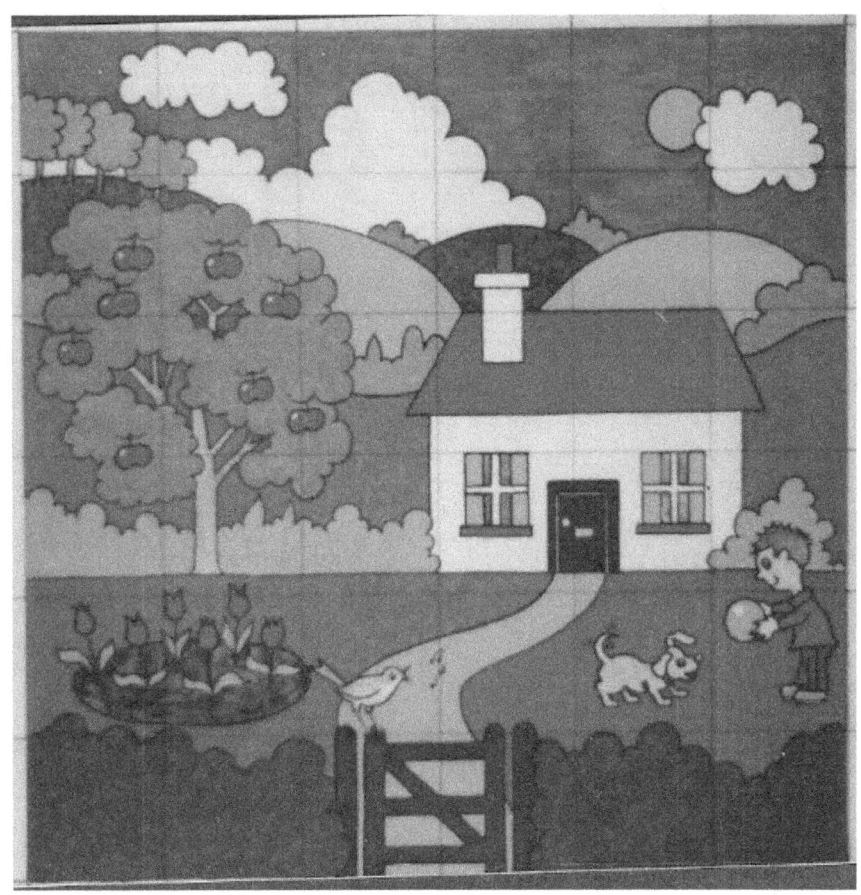

House, date unknown
m: felt pen on paper

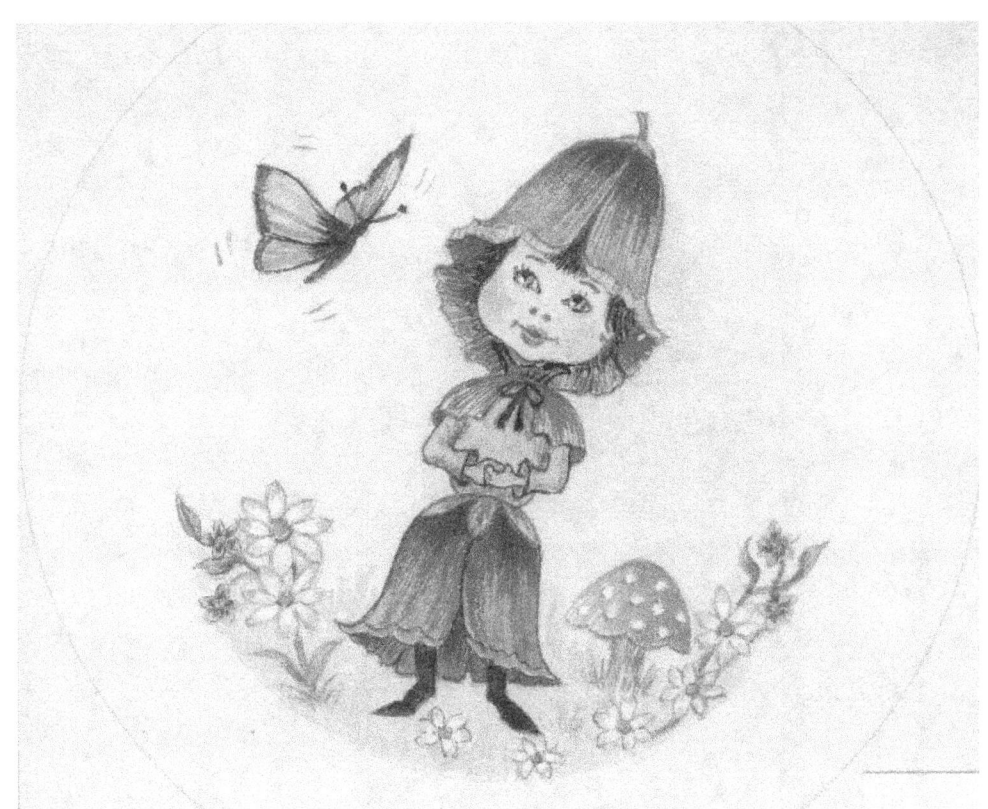

Pixie, date unknown
m: Pastel on paper

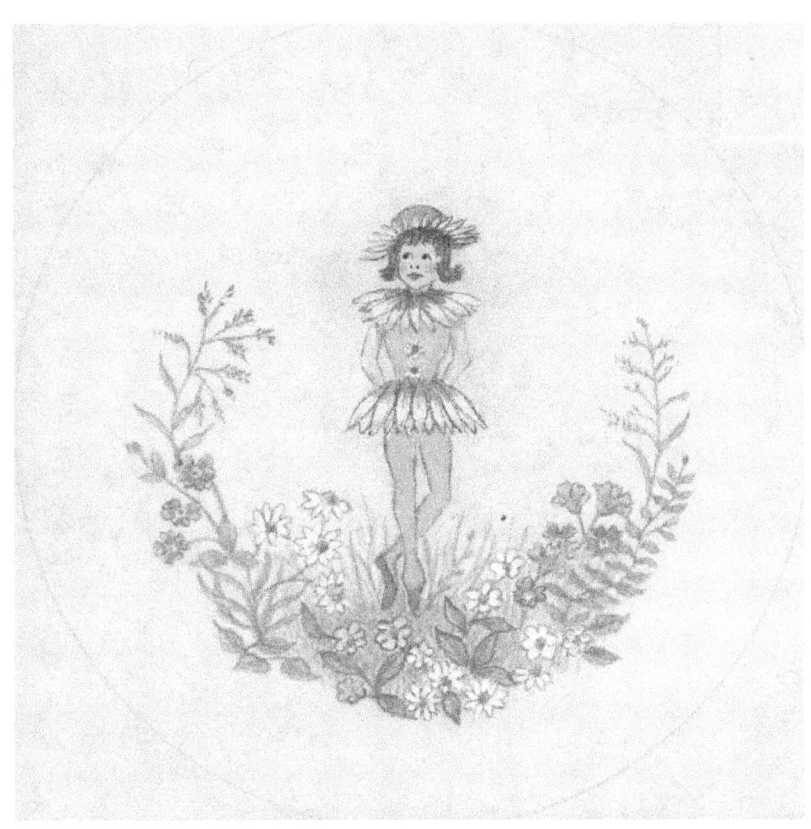

Pixie, date unknown
m: pastel on paper

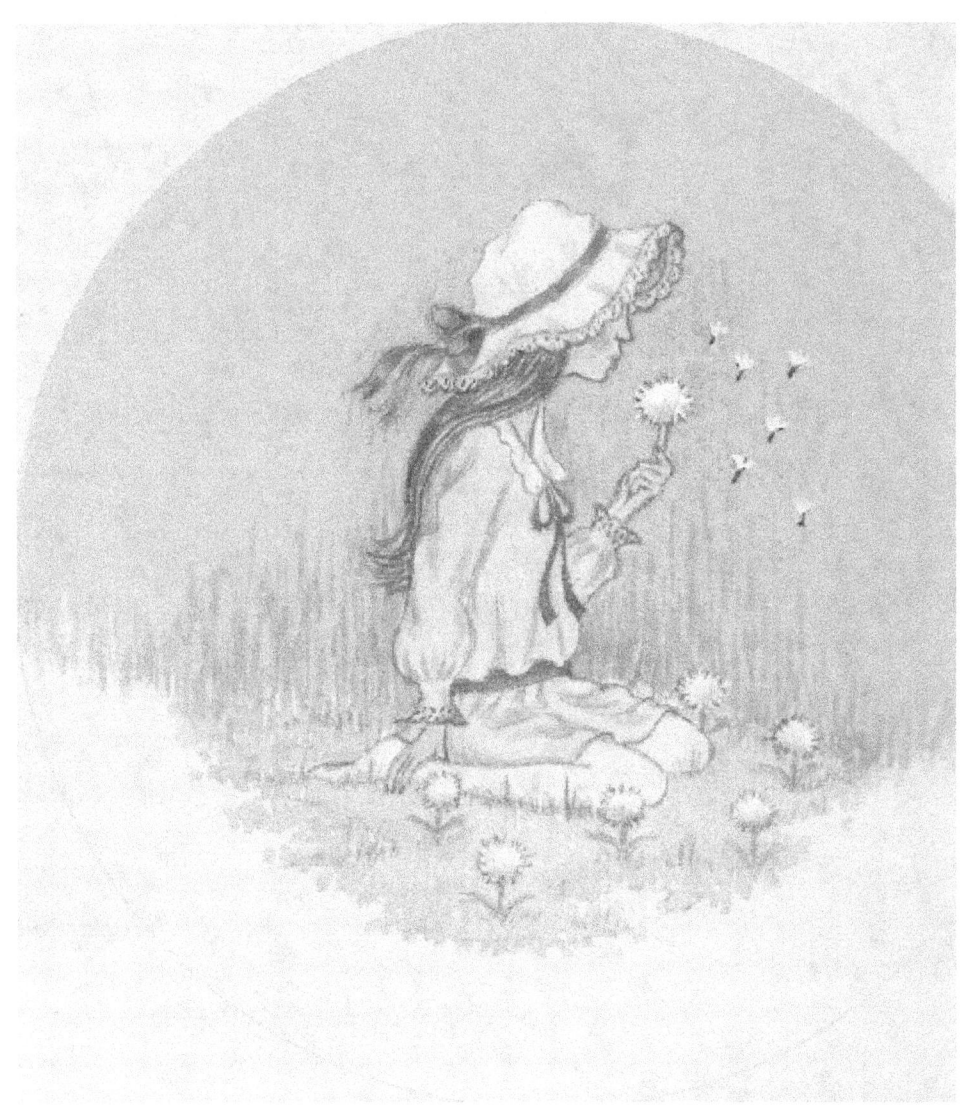

Young girl, date unknown
m: pastel on paper

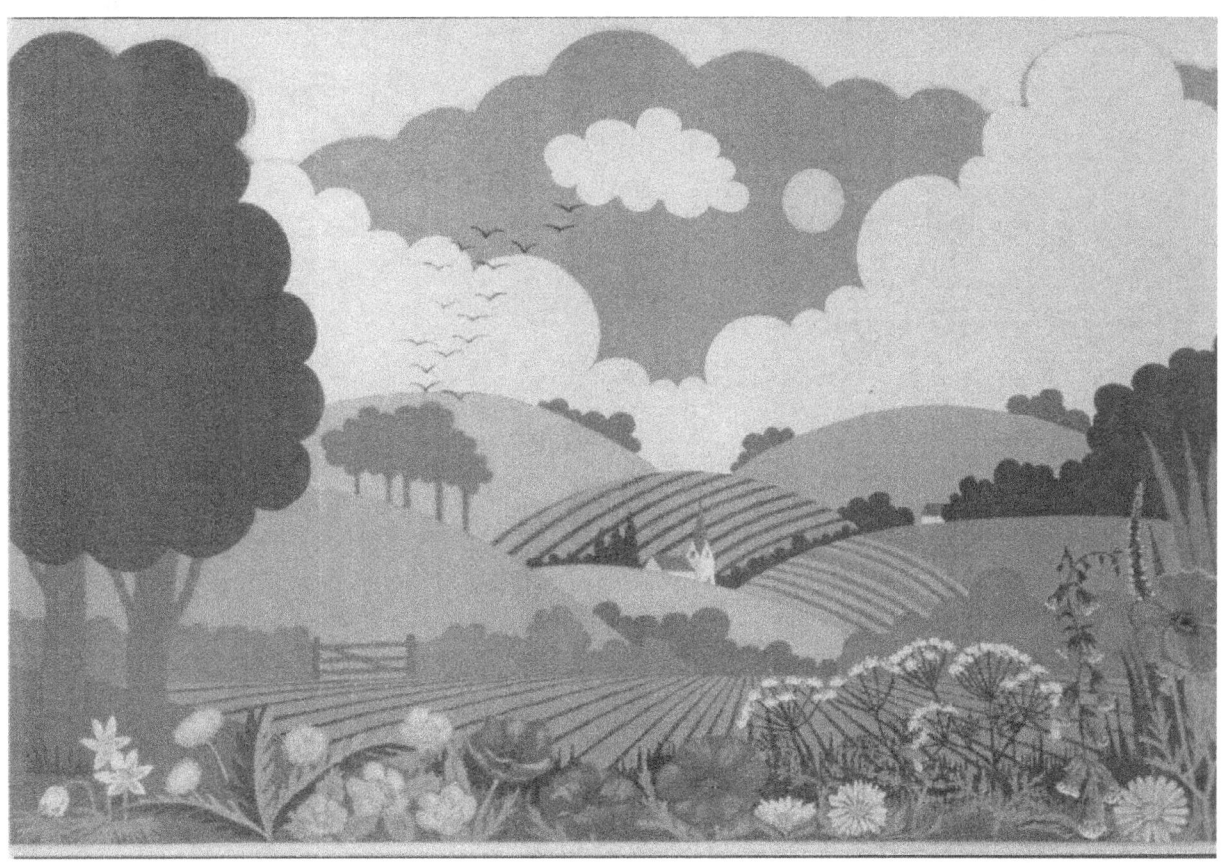

Country Scene, date unknown

m: felt pen on paper

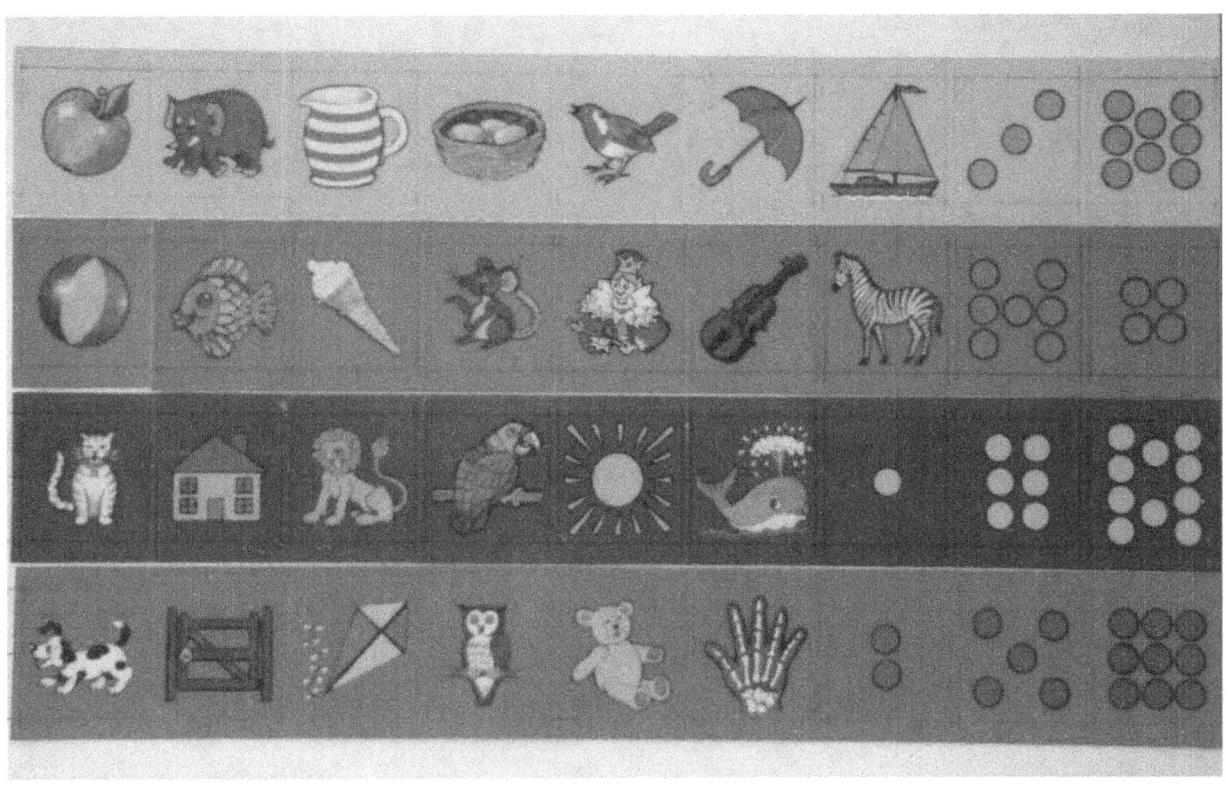

Game pieces, date unknown

m: felt pen on paper

7 STUDIES AND STILL LIFES

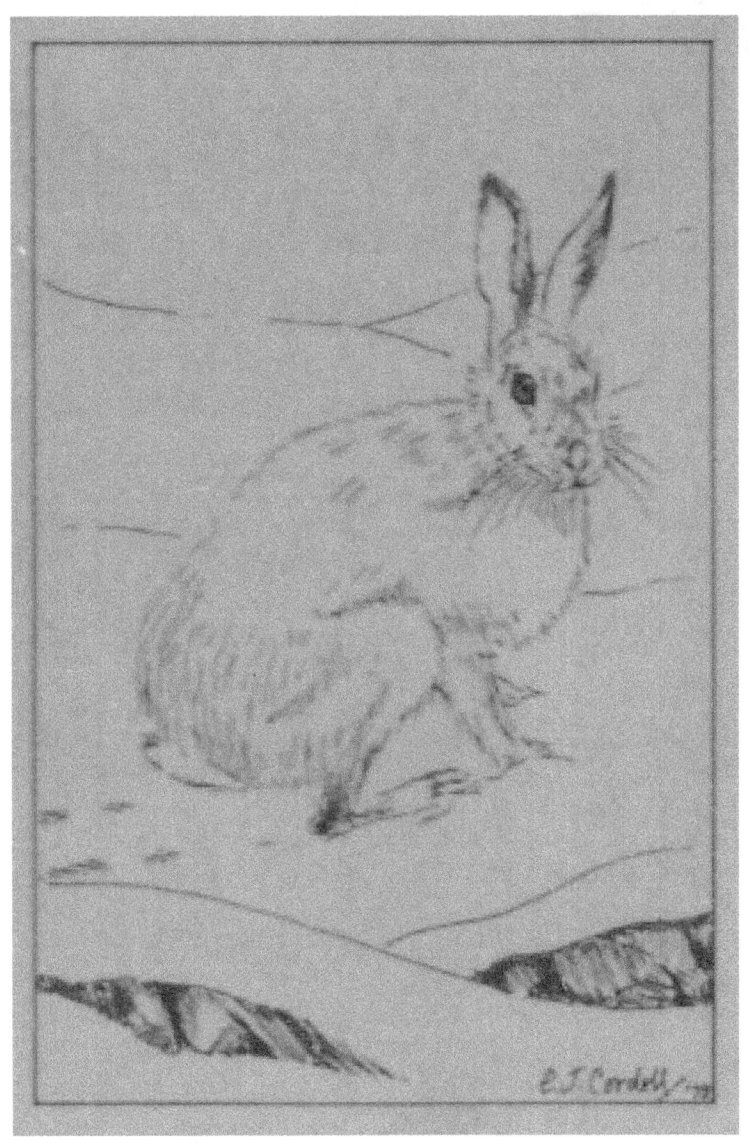

Hare, 1979

m: ink pen on paper

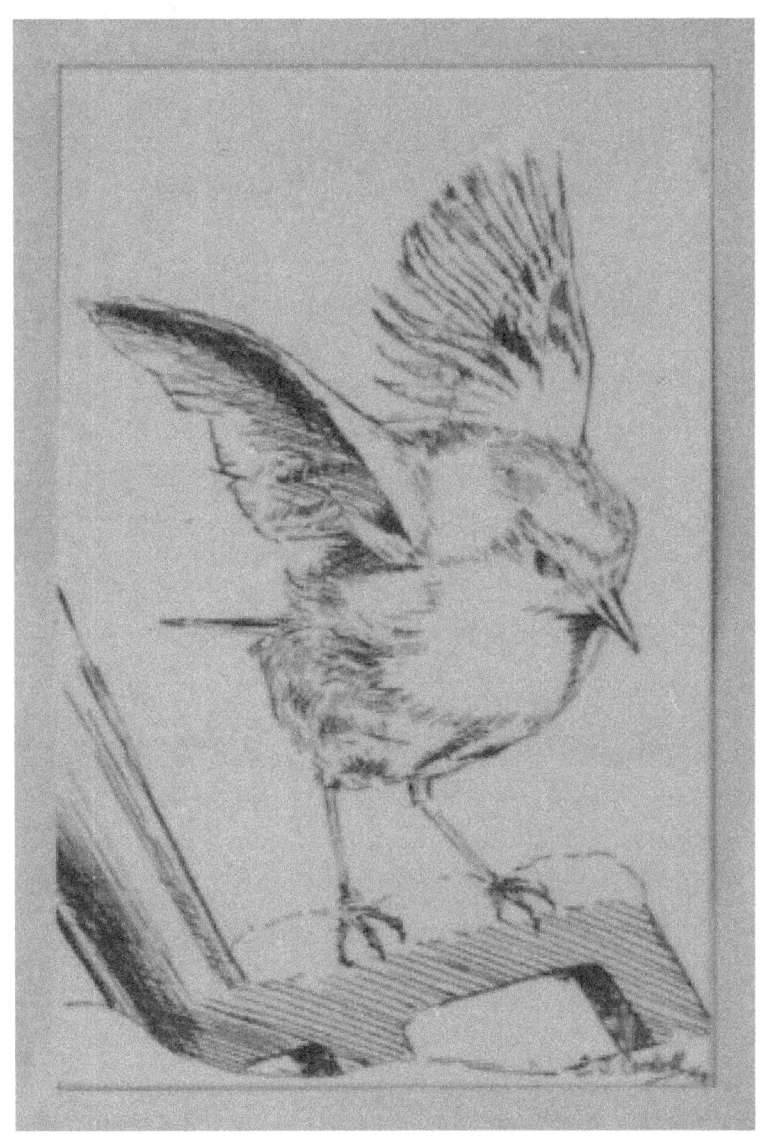

Robin, 1979

m: ink pen on paper

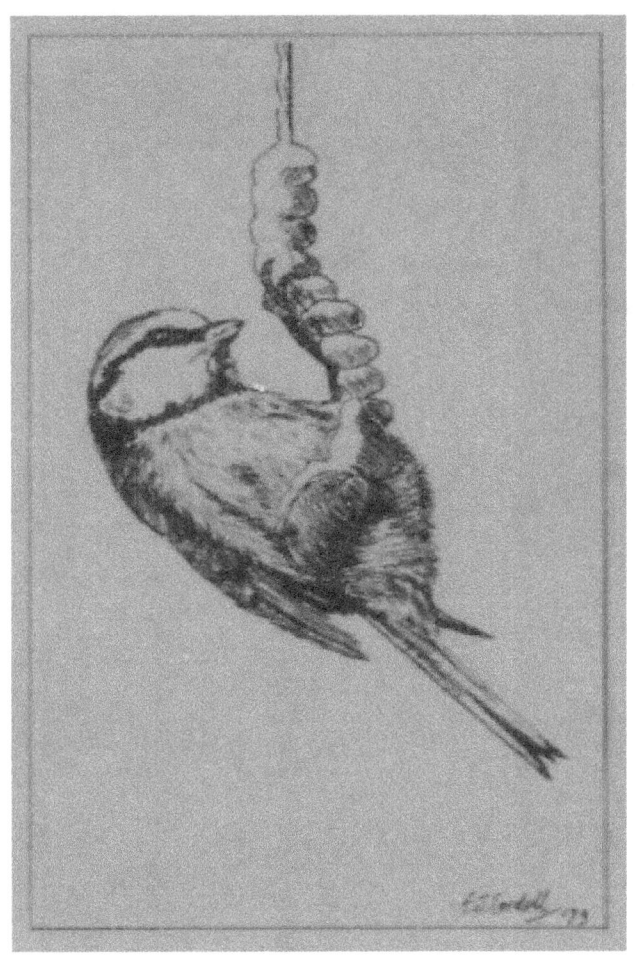

Blue tit, 1979

m: ink pen on paper

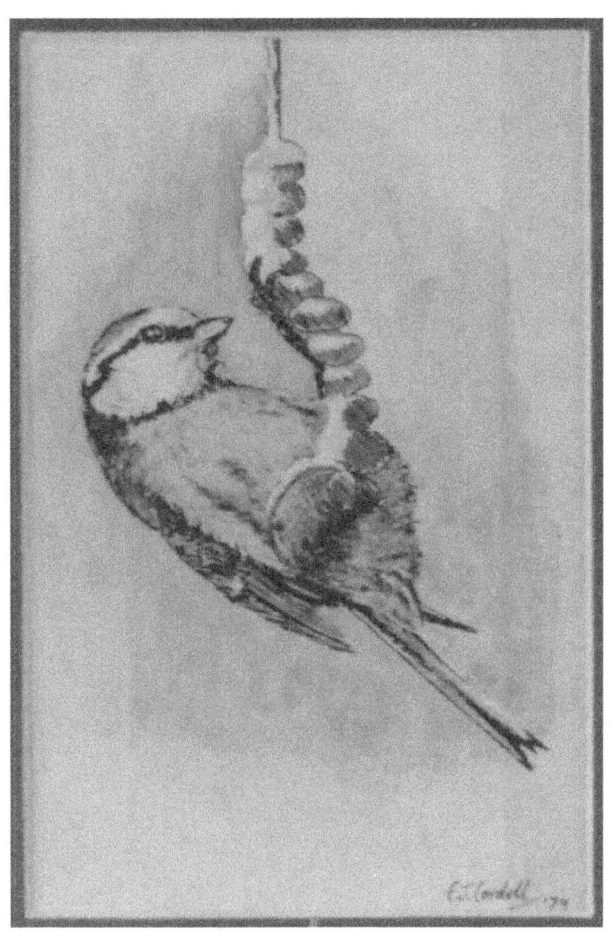

Blue tit, 1979

m: watercolour on paper

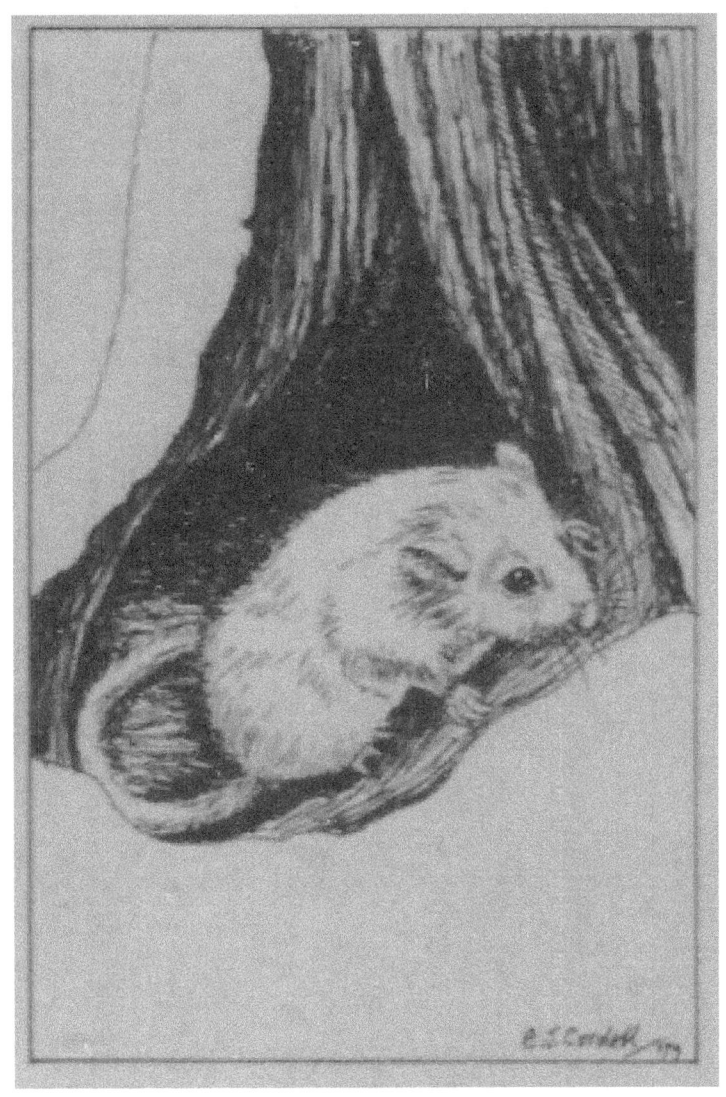

Dormouse, 1979

m: ink pen on paper

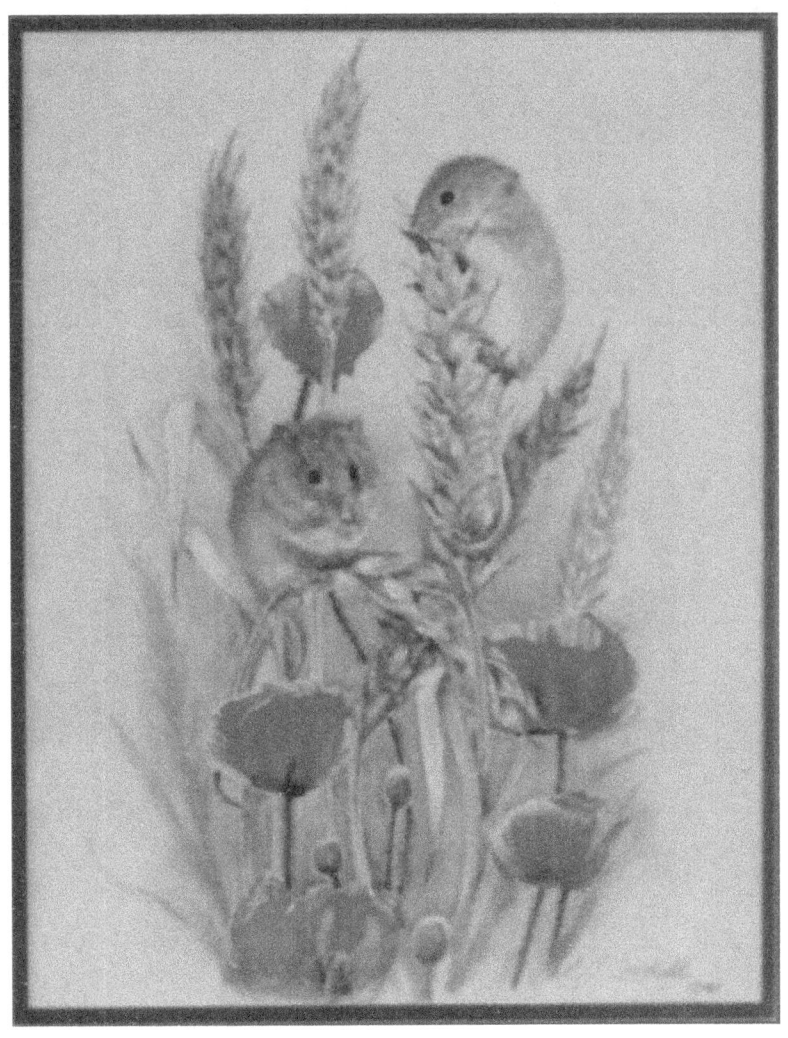

Harvest mice, 1980

m: watercolour on paper

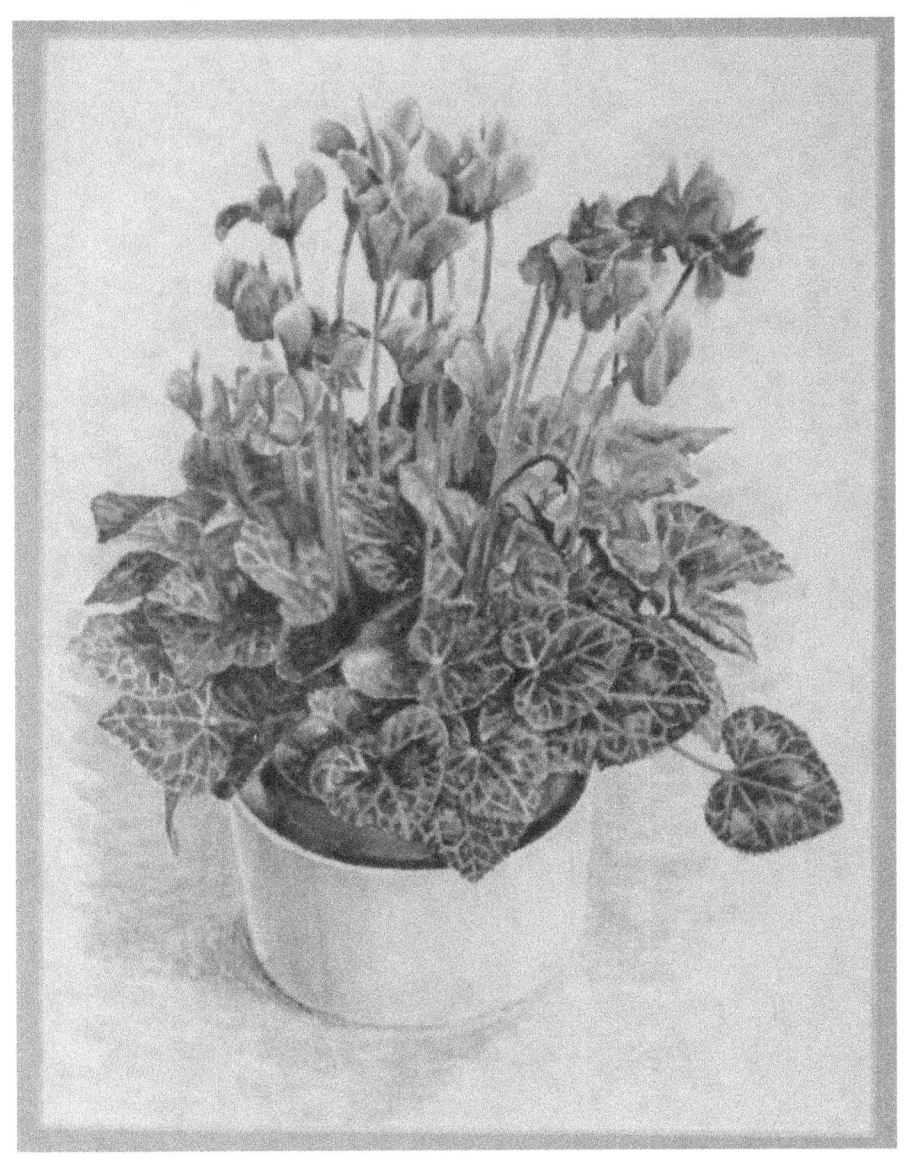

Cyclamen, 1990

m: watercolour on paper

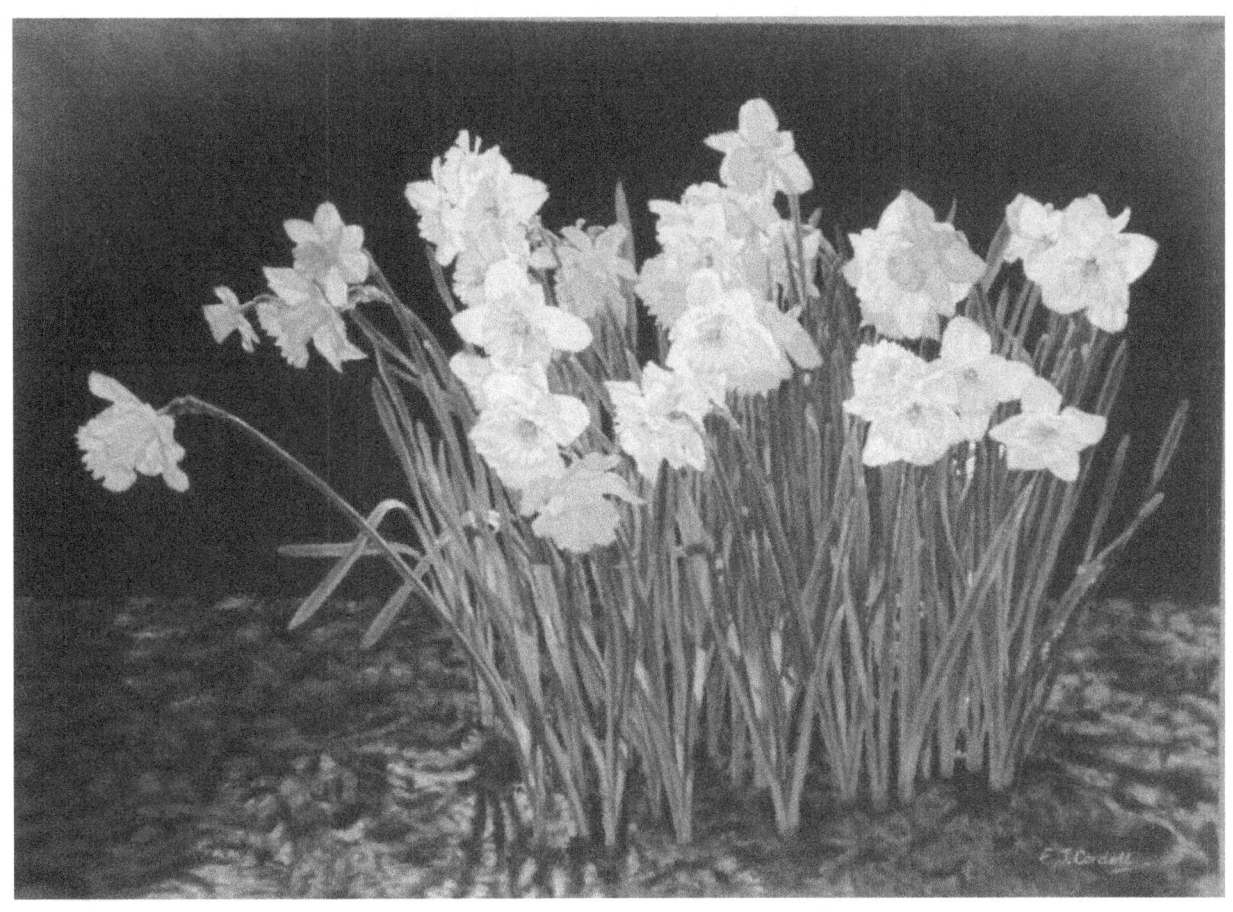

Daffodils, 1992

m: pastel on paper

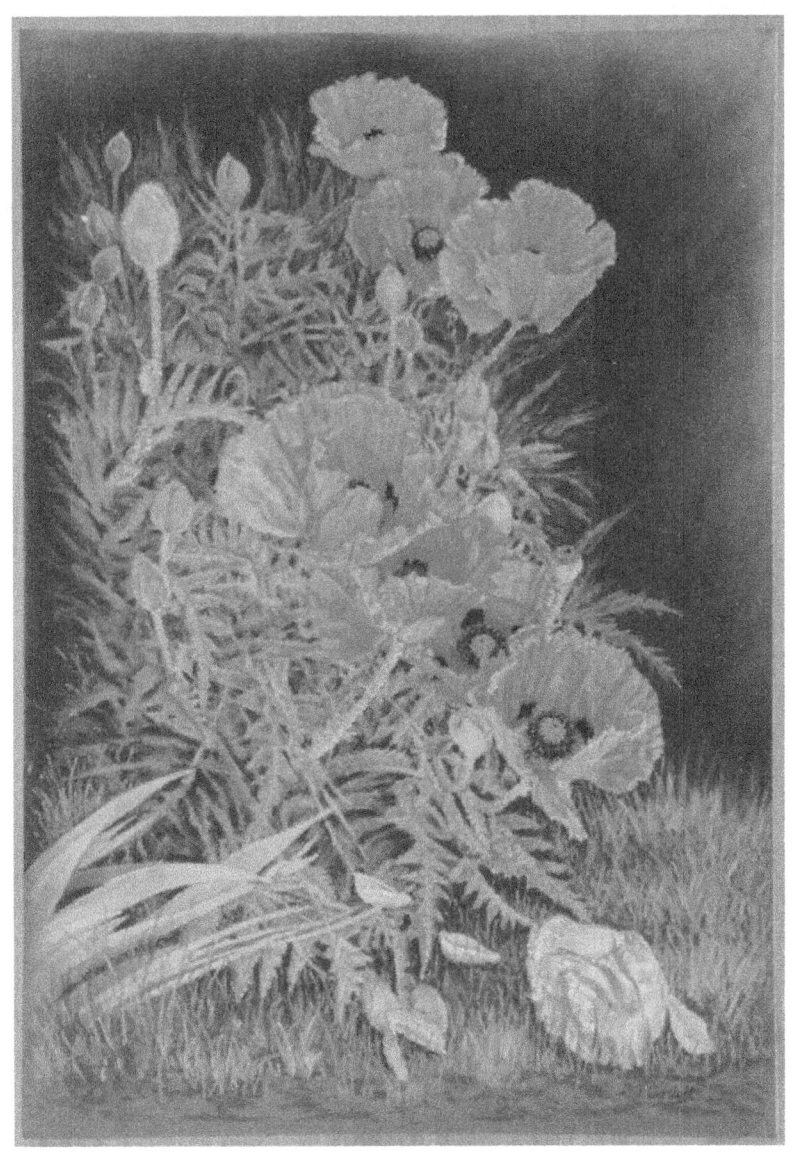

Poppies, 1995

m: pastel on paper

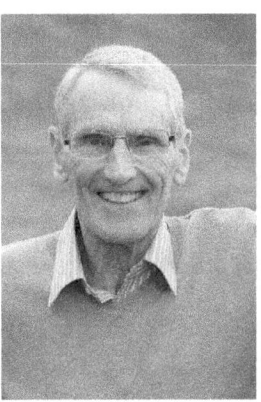

ABOUT THE AUTHOR

Edward John Cordell - affectionately known as Ted to all his family and friends, and Teddy to his much loved youngest sisters, Kay and Gwen - was born in Hook, near Surbiton, Surrey, on 8 June 1939, the eldest child, and only son, of Edward and Muriel Cordell.

His early years were spent in Gordon Road, Ilford, Essex and later Oaks Lane, Newbury Park, Ilford, a new housing estate overlooking farms and fields.

Ted was diagnosed with asthma at the age of 5 years and spent some of his education at a school which emphasized fresh air and care.   He later attended William Torbitt School in Newbury Park from which he obtained, at the age of 13 years, a pass to Ilford County High School.   During sixth form, after a visit to the Design Centre, Haymarket, London, and having shown much interest and talent in the field of art, Ted was accepted into the Central School of Arts and Crafts, London, qualifying with a National Diploma for Design and Dip. CSAC.

He met his sweetheart, Eileen, at St Peter's Church Youth Club, Newbury Park and, after marrying on 10 September 1966, they moved to Chelmsford, Essex where they settled into married life and started a family.

In 1970, Bill Ashton and Ted formed Ashton & Cordell Associates designing for various companies including Prestige and Hymac. In the field of lighting design, one of his designs was chosen by an Arabian Sheik for use in his new palace. Ted took great pride in his work placing equal emphasis on aesthetics and functionality.

It was around this time that Ted was elected a member of the Society of Industrial Artists and Designers.

In the spring of 1973, Ted and Eileen decided to move the family to Pembury, near Tunbridge Wells in Kent, in search of better schools and prospects for their children and also to make contact between the business partners easier. The decision to move proved to be a wise one with both the family and the business partnership flourishing as a result. The business stood the test of time, lasting well into the 1990s, ending only with the retirement of both partners.

Ted continued to paint landscapes, family portraits and pet portraits well into retirement and in October 1997, with the help of the Tunbridge Wells Library and Museum curator, he launched an exhibition of his art works which was a unanimous success. Sadly, Dupuytren's contracture later robbed him of the ability to draw and paint, but not before he created some truly remarkable pieces of artwork.

Ted's works are much loved by all those fortunate enough to have a piece in their collection.